ISAMBARD KINGDOM BRUNEL

'Brunel' arrives back at Bristol
with broad gauge engine *Iron Duke* on 9 March 2006.
SS GREAT BRITAIN TRUST

From the publisher of

Author: Robin Jones
Design: Anita Tams-Waters
Cover design: Darren Hendley
Reprographics: Michael Baumber
Production Editor: Sarah Lawson
Publishing Director: Malcolm Wheeler
Finance Director: Brian V Hill
Managing Director: Terry Clark

Special thanks to: Brunel 200, SS Great Britain Trust, Great
Western Society and Adrian Knowles; Brunel Engine House
Museum, Brian Sharpe, STEAM – Museum of the Great
Western Railway, Ironbridge Gorge Museums Trust, Broad Gauge
Society, Great Western Trust, Firefly Trust, National Waterfront
Museum, Destination Bristol, Corsham Tourist Information Office,
Fred Kerr and Newton Abbot & GWR Museum.

Published by

Independent publishers since 1885

Media Centre, Morton Way, Horncastle, Lincolnshire
LN9 6JR. Tel: 01507 523456

Printed by
William Gibbons and Son, Wolverhampton

Published April 2006

ISBN: 978-955-0-22126-4
ISBN: 0-9550221-2-6

Isambard Kingdom Brunel's
revolutionary steam ship *Great Western*
in a stormy mid Atlantic, as painted by
Joseph Walter. SS GREAT BRITAIN TRUST

BRUNEL

Rediscover the legend

I sambard Kingdom Brunel. Three names. Three people in one. Born in Portsmouth on 9 April 1806, there was Brunel the great engineer, who would habitually throw out the rulebook of tradition and established practice, and start again with a blank sheet of paper, taking the technology of the day to its limits – and then going another mile.

Then there was Brunel the visionary, who knew that transport technology had the power to change the world, and that he had the ability to deliver those changes.

Finally, there was Brunel the artist – who rarely saw technology as just functional, and strove to entwine the fruits of the Industrial Revolution with the elegance and grace of the neo-classical painter. His bridges, tunnels and railway infrastructure have entered a third century of regular use, and the beauty of their design and structure has rarely been equalled.

The three decades, from the 1830s to the 1850s, saw an explosion of technical excellence, and it was Brunel who in so many cases lit the blue touchpaper.

He did not always get it right first time, and it was left to others to reap the fruits of his many labours. Nevertheless, his actions fast-forwarded the march of progress by several decades.

In 2006, Britain is celebrating the 200th anniversary of Brunel's birth, with a multitude of events large and small, for the family, the steam buff and the academic alike.

It will be a wonderful year, in which Isambard's many legacies will be re-examined – and revisited.

The landmarks will take centre stage, of course: the spectacular Royal Albert Bridge at Saltash, the magnificent glass-roofed terminus of Paddington, Maidenhead bridge with its elliptical arches that many said would never stand up, the stupendous Clifton Suspension Bridge, completed shortly after his death, to his design by a team of admirers, Bristol's original Temple Meads station, the Dawlish sea wall railway route – everyone's favourite section of the national network, and many more.

However, I hope that readers may use this commemorative volume as a travel guide to explore some of the lesser-known delights that he has bequeathed to us: the wonderful Bristol & Exeter Railway station at Bridgwater, the Wilts, Somerset & Weymouth Railway booking office at Bradford-on-Avon, and the lofty Devil's Bridge at Bleadon near Weston-super-Mare, to name but a few.

An excellent starting point is one of London's real hidden gems, the Brunel Engine House Museum at Rotherhithe, and its wonderful displays about the Thames Tunnel through which you can travel by underground train below.

Didcot Railway Centre in Oxfordshire is a must, with its demonstration broad- and mixed-gauge running line and award-winning replica *Fire Fly* locomotive.

Don't miss out STEAM – Museum of the Great Western Railway in Swindon, which takes you on a unique journey through time to tell the story of God's Wonderful Railway and the man who created it, with *North Star*, the engine that made the line work, taking pride of place.

Then there's Bristol's Floating Harbour, one of the world's greatest waterfronts and, with many multi-million-pound development schemes in progress, getting better by the week. The jewel in its crown is, of course, the SS Great Britain, a vessel everyone should visit at least once in their life.

Brunel was the catalyst, which the Industrial Revolution needed to take it further to the next stage. He was by no means the only pioneer of his day, but perhaps more than anyone else, with the aid of the steam engine, provided the link between that great era of discovery and invention, and the modern world.

Why do we remain so fascinated by Brunel and his inventions?

Maybe it is because he symbolises the swashbuckling hero we are all seeking in perpetuity, the person who really does have the power to bring the future to today.

Robin Jones

60

BRUNEL | 1806–2006   CLIFTON SUSPENSION BRIDGE DESIGN

47

BRUNEL | 1806–2006   PSS GREAT EASTERN

42

BRUNEL | 1806–2006   PADDINGTON STATION

40

BRUNEL | 1806–2006   BOX TUNNEL

68

BRUNEL | 1806–2006   MAIDENHEAD BRIDGE

MARC BRUNEL

The revolution begins

What I find most amazing about Marc Isambard Brunel is that Hollywood has never seen fit to produce a blockbuster movie about him.

His story of world-shaping success has all the ingredients that you might expect from a late-18th century James Bond or Indiana Jones; a larger-than-life character who so often would throw caution to the wind, in the pursuit of a greater goal, regardless of the risks – with a classic fairytale romance thrown in.

Rejecting the life of a priest at an early age and cheating the guillotine, in Scarlet Pimpernel fashion, during the French Revolution – as would his future bride – Marc Brunel escaped to the United States, where made his name, before losing his fortune in England and winning it back again.

Not only that, but – most importantly – there would be a futuristic tunnel involved along the way – an essential ingredient in most Bond films. This one, however, would not be the fictional big-screen den of some sinister mastermind who wanted to take control of the world, but one which would genuinely change it in more ways than the young Marc could ever have imagined.

Furthermore, he would have a son who would not only follow in his engineering footsteps, but who, nearly two centuries after his birth, would take second place behind Sir Winston Churchill in a nationwide poll to find the greatest Briton of all time, even beating Shakespeare – not bad for someone who was half French.

Marc Brunel was born on 25 April 1769 in the hamlet of Hacqueville, near Rouen in France, the son of a wealthy farmer, Jean Charles Brunel, and his second wife, Marie Victoria Lefevre.

As soon as he could read and write, the young Marc displayed a talent for drawing, mathematics and mechanics.

His father, however, was having none of Marc's aspirations to become an engineer and join the new breed of pioneers spawned by the Industrial Revolution, on the other side of the English Channel.

Jean Charles insisted that his son had a career in the church, and so at the age of 11, he was sent to a seminary in Rouen.

There, the Superior saw that Marc's talents in drawing and woodwork would be better engaged elsewhere, especially as he had no religious leaning. So, it was arranged for him to stay with an elder cousin, Madam Carpentier, whose husband, a retired ship's captain, had become the American consul in Rouen.

While living with the Carpentiers, Marc attended the Royal College in Rouen, and excelled at mathematics, geometry, mechanics and drawing.

His scholarly success led him to a place as a cadet on the naval frigate *Marechal de Castries* and a six-year career at sea.

...As soon as he could read and write, the young Marc displayed a talent for drawing, mathematics and mechanics...

In January 1792, Marc returned home to find his native country embroiled in the worst excesses of the French Revolution. A Norman, and a staunch royalist sympathiser, he was at odds with the aims of the murderous Jacobins.

When, in January 1793, he made scathing remarks in a speech about the brutal Robespierre, during a visit to the Café de l'Echelle in Paris, he was lucky to escape a howling, revolutionary mob by the skin of his teeth, hiding in an inn for the night.

In Rouen, he found that the Carpentiers had a new guest, 17-year-old Sophia Kingdom.

She was the youngest of 16 children of Portsmouth naval-contractor, William Kingdom, who had died some years before. Her family had decided to send her to France with a friend, Monsieur de Longuemarre, and his English wife.

When a friend of the de Longuemarres was murdered by a mob for playing a royalist tune at a piano, the couple fled back to England, leaving Sophia behind, as she had been too ill to travel. At the Carpentiers' house, she fell in love with Marc Brunel.

Feeling the heat because of his sympathies with the Ancien Régime in France, and with Rouen in Jacobin hands, Marc fled the country for the USA, alone, but with the elaborate help of friends, amid justifiable fears for his safety.

Left: The fall of the Bastille on 14 July 1789. The ensuing Reign of Terror not only brought royalist Marc Brunel and his future wife together, but led to him fleeing France and making his fortune as an engineer in New York.

Opposite: Samuel Drummond's portrait of Marc Brunel in later life, showing the Thames Tunnel, his greatest achievement.
BRUNEL ENGINE HOUSE

He obtained a passport, after falsely claiming he was buying grain for the Navy, sailed away on the aptly named Liberty, and then established himself as a surveyor, architect and civil engineer in New York.

There, Marc built the old Bowery Theatre, in its day, the largest theatre in North America. He also built many other buildings, including an arsenal and a cannon foundry, as well as improving the defences between Staten and Long Island, and surveying a canal between Lake Champlain and the Hudson River at Albany.

He eventually took US citizenship and became chief engineer to the city of New York.

One of his designs won the competition for a new US capitol building to be built in Washington DC, but it was found too costly to implement and another plan was chosen instead.

While Marc prospered on the far side of the pond, Sophia remained in grave peril for her life.

Following the execution of Louis XVI and Marie Antoinette, Britain declared war on France, and all British nationals were imprisoned. Sophia found herself in a convent at Gravelines, near Calais, which had been turned into a makeshift prison – complete with a guillotine. This, despite representations from the Carpentiers and Republican families, whose children she had taught English.

Sophia was not released until July 1794, when Robespierre was overthrown. The following year, she returned to her family's London home.

In February 1799, Marc decided to leave America and start again in England – perhaps driven by an all-consuming desire to renew his acquaintance with

Sophia, whom he had never forgotten.

They were reunited in spring that year, and were married at the parish church of St Andrew in Holborn, on 1 November 1799, setting up their first home in Bedford Street, Bloomsbury.

Marc had certainly not left his entrepreneurial spirit behind him in New York, in the first few weeks of his arrival in Britain; he had filed a patent for a 'duplicating, writing and drawing machine'.

However, his big break came when the Government awarded him a £17,000 contract, after accepting his plans for mechanising the manufacture of pulley blocks for ships, which until then had been made by hand.

By 1808, a total of 43 machines of his design were installed in the naval dockyard at Portsmouth, where they became one of the earliest examples of all-mechanised production in the world.

With the machines, 10 men could do the job previously done by 100, and furthermore, Marc's blocks were superior in quality and consistency to the handmade predecessors.

The Brunels moved with their new daughter, Sophia, to a small terraced house in Portsea, near Portsmouth, from where Marc supervised the six-year project to build the block-making factory.

It was at this house in the early hours of 9 April 1806

that Isambard Kingdom Brunel was born.

Marc went on to design great, steam-powered machines for sawing and bending timber, some of which were also taken up by the Navy. He also worked on devices for stocking knitting and printing.

Horrified at the condition of the feet of soldiers returning from the Corunna campaign in 1809, Marc invented a series of machines to mass-produce boots and shoes, filing a patent the following year. His idea proved so successful that the Government asked him to expand production.

At Chatham's dockyard, Marc installed one of his sawmills, served by a rope-hauled railway with rails that were 7ft apart – much, much more of that later.

His success in the woodcutting field led to him joining forces in 1807, with a Mr Farthing, to set up a sawmill business in Battersea, and so Marc moved back to London with his family to oversee it.

While the block-making operation was a success, the Navy proved to be slow at paying, and the Brunels needed a more regular income. Like everything that had gone before it, the sawmill was a success – Marc supplied the technology, Farthing the finance and business acumen.

All went well until Farthing retired in 1813, and then, without his hand on the tiller, the firm's finances fell into neglect.

The next year, the sawmills were all but destroyed in a fire, and Marc, when he finally looked at the bank balance, found the firm's finances to be far worse than he had thought.

Just to add to his financial woes, his army boot factory was dealt a major blow by Wellington's victory at Waterloo in 1815.

The Government decided to reduce the size of the Army, and Marc was left with a consignment of unwanted boots. He had to sell them off cheap to fund the rebuilding of the sawmills.

In the meantime, Marc, who had been elected to the Royal Society in 1814, had spent much time devising a series of new inventions, many of which were far less successful than his block-making equipment and saws.

In 1812, he experimented with steam navigation on the Thames, to no avail. He devised a series of compressed air engines, which turned out to be impracticable, designed a knitting machine, which nobody would buy, and entered into fruitless talks with the Russian Tsar, Alexander I, for a suspension bridge across the Neva River in St Petersburg.

Marc then came up with a handheld copying press, a device, which could make decorative packaging from tin foil and also began work on a rotary press for the *Times* newspaper.

Disaster hit in 1820, when, after years of continual, habitual neglect of the financial, rather than, technological side of his ailing business empire, his bankers, Sykes & Co, were now insolvent, and nobody would honour his cheques.

Marc and Sophia could no longer pay their debts and on 14 May 1821, were hauled off to the King's Bench debtors' prison, where they spent three months – until influential friends, led by the Duke of Wellington, managed to persuade the Government to stump up £5000, lest the inventor's services be lost to Russia, where the Tsar had shown renewed interest in his Neva River scheme.

Able to pay off his crippling debts at last, Marc resumed his career in a far more humble manner, becoming a consulting engineer in an office at 29 Poultry, in the City of London.

Young Isambard Kingdom Brunel had, in the meantime, been groomed by his father to take over the business.

Marc taught his son drawing and geometry, before sending him to Dr Morell's boarding school in Hove. While at the school, Isambard carried out a survey of the town and made many drawings of the houses there.

Young Isambard Kingdom Brunel had, in the meantime, been groomed by his father to take over the business.

The machine ran off without him, at 8mph, and terrified the rector...

At the age of 14, he was sent to France to finish his schooling at the College of Caen, in Normandy, and progressed from there, to the Lycée Henri-Quatre in Paris. He also studied at the Institution de M Massin.

His father had also arranged for him to have an apprenticeship under Louis Breguet, the world-famous maker of clocks, chronometers and other scientific instruments.

While his father underwent what the family described as his 'misfortune', Isambard had been abroad, not returning to England until August 1822, at the age of 16.

He immediately took up work in his father's office, working alongside him on designs for a cannon-boring mill for the Netherlands government, the rotary printing press – amongst much else, including two suspension bridges for the French Government for the Île de Bourbon (Reunion) off Mauritius.

The father-and-son team worked on more mechanical engineering designs, and came up with the first double-acting marine engine, which set on course a chain of events, which would lead Isambard to worldwide fame and glory.

Two years before Isambard had been born, in 1804, a Cornish mining engineer named Richard Trevithick had sown the seeds of a transport revolution which would change the face of, and shrink, the globe: the first railway locomotive.

While Ironbridge is widely regarded today as the cradle of the Industrial Revolution, necessity was very much the mother of invention in the wilds of Cornwall, where the landscape so beloved by holidaymakers today, resembled the Black Country or South Wales coalfields in their heyday, being littered with the engine houses, processing mills and slag heaps of various tin, copper, lead and arsenic mines.

The biggest problem for mining was keeping the tunnels free of water, and some of those in Cornwall stretched out beneath the sea. It was the stationary steam engine, which provided a satisfactory means of pumping out water so that the mines could be worked safely.

All well and good, but there was the difficulty in transporting large, steam-engine components from manufacturers like Boulton & Watt of Birmingham, to the Duchy for assembly - Cornwall was never connected to the canal network, which had made the Industrial Revolution 'happen' and its mining areas lay in hilly terrain that were mainly accessed only by sea.

But, what if a machine could move by itself to the site where it was to work, instead of being dragged there by horses?

Furthermore, what if it could pull other machines, and maybe even carry people?

Trevithick, who was born on 13 April 1771, did not invent the first machine that could move itself using the power of steam.

That honour goes to Austro-Hungarian army officer Nicholas Joseph Cugnot, who wanted to devise a more efficient means of moving heavy artillery than horses, resulting in the world's first steam tractor, which appeared in 1769, with a refined prototype displayed in Paris the following year.

Cugnot's invention was a clumsy and overweight device, with appalling steering, or lack of it, and which could operate for only 20 minutes before it needed to cool down and have fresh water added – not exactly an asset in battle. His work came to an abrupt end when his weighty machine overturned in a busy street.

Meanwhile in Britain, Scotsman William Murdoch had been experimenting with steam traction while working for Boulton & Watt as its Cornish agent, and in 1784, his first working model hauled a wagon around a room, inside his Redruth home.

Murdoch then gave an infamous outdoor trial to a 19in-long, three-wheeled steam carriage one night along the narrow lane leading to the town's church. The machine ran off without him, at 8mph, and terrified the rector, who believed that the devil was about to attack him.

Undeterred, Murdoch built an improved model and apparently a further two carriages as well – and they were seen not only by the townsfolk of Redruth but, also by the young Richard Trevithick.

However, Murdoch's work ceased towards the end of the 1790s, and he is better remembered as the man who invented gaslight, using it to light his Redruth home.

Trevithick, however, was working on increasing steam pressure, so that he could make smaller engines. He quickly realised that if a much-smaller engine could power a machine or pump, then it could also be capable of being adapted to drive itself.

Forming a partnership with Andrew Vivian, he launched his own steam carriage on Christmas Eve 1801, when it successfully climbed Camborne Hill under its own power.

Several onlookers ecstatically jumped aboard and rode on it – making it the world's first motorcar.

There was jubilation all round and those involved in the escapade celebrated at the inn at the top – leaving the locomotive to burn out.

Two subsequent experiments with steam carriages in London proved unsuccessful, purely because of the unsurfaced roads of the day, so Trevithick sought a

It was unlikely that Trevithick ever envisaged a national network of railways...

Above: The bust of Isambard Kingdom Brunel in Rotherhithe's excellent museum in the Brunel Engine House.
ROBIN JONES

Opposite right: Isambard Kingdom Brunel, as painted by his brother-in-law JC Horsley, in 1833.
BRUNEL ENGINE HOUSE

medium, which could support their great weight – the railway.

In 1802, he began work on building a railway locomotive for use at Coalbrookdale ironworks in Shropshire, near the site of the world's first iron bridge, although it was not believed to have run in public. He was then asked to install a high-pressure locomotive to run from Penydarren ironworks near Merthyr Tydfil, along the horse-drawn tram road that linked the works to the Glamorganshire Canal at Abercynon wharf, and jumped at the opportunity.

On February 21 1804, Trevithick's engine hauled a rake of loaded wagons, plus 70 men, along the full length of the tramway, immediately earning him the accolade of the world's first railway locomotive engineer. However, the cast-iron plates, which formed the rails, cracked under the weight of the engine in several places.

Trevithick then built a similar locomotive at Gateshead for use on the Wylam Colliery waggonway in 1805, but the mine owners decided not to buy it, probably because their railway's rails were made of wood, so, it was converted to blow the furnace, as a stationary engine.

In 1808, Trevithick turned out his last steam railway locomotive, Catch-Me-Who-Can, which ran on a circle of track in fairground fashion for public gaze - ironically very near to the site of the future Euston station. With its carriage, it became the world's first, steam passenger train.

Trevithick made little money from his railway experiments, and turned away from steam traction for the last time, sadly accepting that the horse and cart, whether on rails, roads or a canal towpath, still reigned supreme.

It was unlikely that Trevithick ever envisaged a national network of railways; he merely intended his engines to replace horses on the short tramways, which served canals, harbours and other transhipment points for industrial products or supplies.

Not everyone was as pessimistic. In 1812, the need for a serious alternative to horses arose out of the relentless demands for their supply and use in the continuing war between Britain and Napoleon.

England's north-east, like Cornwall, had no connection to the national waterway network, so, another form of bulk transport was needed, and fast.

Christopher Blackett, who owned Wylam Colliery, failed to persuade Trevithick to have one last attempt at railway engines. Meanwhile William Hedley and Timothy Hackworth obliged, and with the aid of engine-wright Jonathan Forster, built the legendary eight-wheeled, eight-ton Puffing Billy for the mine's tramway system, drawing much inspiration from Trevithick's designs.

George Stephenson, who was later to become a close friend of Isambard Brunel, built his first engine in 1815, and the world's first steam-powered public line, the Stockton and Darlington Railway, which Stephenson helped engineer, opened in 1825.

Among Brunel's circle of friends was another Cornishman, Sir Humphrey Davy, a chemist who discovered the anaesthetic effect of nitrous oxide (laughing gas) and invented a safety lamp for use in coal mines, allowing deep seams to be mined, despite the presence of methane. Considered to be Britain's leading scientist, in 1812 he was knighted by George III. Davy and his assistant, Michael Faraday, found that several gases could be liquefied by a combination of low temperature and very high pressure, and in 1823 Marc

In 1812, the need for a serious alternative to horses arose out of the relentless demands for their supply and use in the continuing war between Britain and Napoleon.

Brunel became convinced that their discoveries could form the basis of a more efficient type of engine to rival the steam variety.

For much of the ensuing decade, Marc and Isambard spent their time experimenting with pressurised carbonic gas, in a bid to break new ground in a fertile age for new inventions, to produce what they called the Gaz Engine, but despite throwing £15,000 of the father's money at the project, it could not be made to work. This would be a rare example of a Brunel failure, despite their perseverance.

Railways would have to wait, however, for in 1823, Marc Brunel began work on what would be his greatest project of all – the Thames Tunnel.

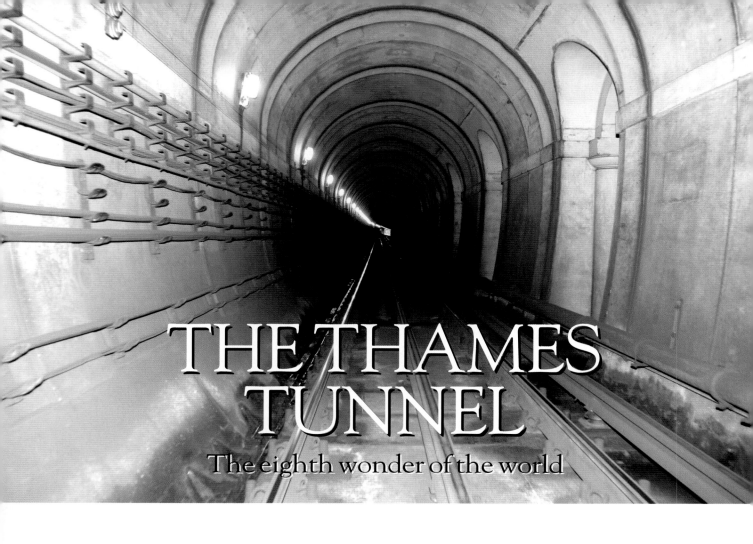

THE THAMES TUNNEL
The eighth wonder of the world

We Britons are by and large a modest bunch, maybe too modest for our own good. For instance, had it been a US citizen who had invented the world's first steam locomotive, and not Richard Trevithick, we would never hear the last of it.

Our nation oozes heritage out of every orifice, yet so much of it we have passed by, or let disappear without trace, before we realise its importance.

In a back street in London's Rotherhithe stands a small, yellow-stone industrial building, which stands out only because it has a tall chimney and unlike the surrounding properties, is not a domestic dwelling.

Those intent on visiting the capital to see the Tower of London, Buckingham Palace or St Paul's Cathedral would not give it a second glance, and in any case, Rotherhithe is well off the beaten tourist track.

Yet, in so many ways, this structure is far more important than any of the aforementioned, at least in terms of the development of the modern world.

Now known as the Brunel Museum (formerly the Brunel Engine House), this humble building in Railway Avenue should be a first port of call, for it is a veritable mine of discovery – if only for the fact that it was built to drain the world's first public, underwater tunnel.

Today tunnels beneath the Thames are commonplace, and building one would hardly grab the headlines. We have tunnels for underground trains, road traffic, essential services like gas, water and electricity, telecommunications and even a secret network of corridors between government buildings, it is believed.

However, back in the 19th century, when Britain led the world in technology, the Thames Tunnel was hailed as its eighth wonder, and with much justification.

To gauge its importance, we have to imagine ourselves back in the London of 200 years ago, when the sole means of crossing the river was by way of the medieval London Bridge, or by using ferrymen.

The first enclosed docks opened in 1802 on the Isle of Dogs, and within 20 years it had been followed by the East India Docks at Blackwall, London Docks at Wapping, and Surrey Docks at Rotherhithe. Downstream from the Tower of London, both sides of the river were crammed with warehouses and factories, but the river placed a major stumbling block to lines of communication and trade.

The volume of traffic on the water caused much congestion, and it was obvious that a new physical crossing would be needed. However, a bridge would have to be high enough to clear the masts of ships, and the technology for a lifting structure on the lines of the later Tower Bridge had not yet been developed.

Thoughts turned towards the building of a tunnel, but no blueprint for the construction of one was readily available.

It was said that in the ancient world, the Assyrian queen Semiramis had the River Euphrates at Babylon diverted, so a tunnel could be built beneath it, for her personal use, and some believed that the Romans bored beneath the sea off Marseille.

In recent times, tunnels under the sea for mining purposes, off the west coast of Cornwall and beneath the

estuary of the River Tyne had been hacked through rock, but these were not built for public use and did not have to contend with the soft ground normally found under riverbeds. Master that single problem – and a Thames tunnel could be built.

In 1798, Ralph Dodd, the designer of the Grand Surrey Canal, proposed a 900-yard tunnel between Gravesend and Tilbury and obtained sufficient money to sink a shaft, but was not able to raise further funds after geological problems were encountered.

Four years later, Robert Vazie drew up plans for a shorter tunnel on the narrower part of the river between Rotherhithe and Limehouse, and joined forces with none other than fellow Cornish mining expert, Richard Trevithick, to build it under the auspices of the Thames Archway Company, which was duly founded in 1805.

Work on digging a 5ft-high pilot tunnel at a depth of 76ft feet began at Rotherhithe in August 1807 and progressed at the rate of 6ft per day, speeding up when Trevithick took sole charge.

After the tunnel crossed the halfway point, a layer of rock was encountered, beyond which lay quicksand – which in turn brought water flooding into the tunnel, causing part of the roof to collapse.

Undeterred, the miners pressed on, draining the tunnel after blocking the hole. There were more inrushes of water, however, including one, which nearly drowned Trevithick on 26 January 1808, after the low-tide mark on the north bank of the Thames had been reached.

Trevithick, who left only when the water was up to his neck, repaired the breach by dumping clay onto the riverbed before pumping the tunnel dry.

To counteract such problems, he devised a new method by which the tunnel would be built from above. The miners would work inside a series of cofferdams and lay a tunnel, comprising of cast-iron sections inside their trench.

However, it had never been done before, and his company's directors and financial backers were having none of it, instead offering a prize of £500 to anyone who could find another means of finishing the tunnel. When none of the 49 offered solutions were deemed workable, the tunnel was abandoned, with less than 200ft to go.

In 1818, however, Marc Brunel patented a tunnelling shield; a device that made it possible to safely bore through water-bearing strata such as the offending quicksand.

While Marc had been engaged with his sawmill at Chatham Dockyard, he studied the destructive shipworm, *teredo navalis*, which ate its way through timber with its hard, horny head, leaving a coating

around the 'tunnel' it had gnawed.

He had already looked at the possibility of a tunnel under the River Neva for the Russian Tsar, and in doing so had brought himself up to speed with the technical problems that would be involved.

His revolutionary shield consisted of 12 separate numbered cast-iron frames, comprising a total of 36 cells in which a miner could work independently of the others.

The propulsion for the device was provided by a screw, which drove the shield forward in 4.5-inch steps, the width of a brick.

The frames with the odd numbers were worked first, and as each board was replaced, it was braced with polling screws against the adjacent cell. When all the boards had been worked down, the shield could move forward and the screws were replaced. The main frame would be worked forward by the use of screw jacks bracing against brickwork behind. Each foot of tunnel required 5500 bricks to be laid.

Brunel's 1818 patent had detailed a circular boring shield, with long rotary cutting blades at the front to

Left: As the tunnel is an International Landmark Site, when it was refurbished in the 1990s, four of the original arches were preserved as built. BRUNEL ENGINE HOUSE

Top: The River Thames above the Thames Tunnel. ROBIN JONES

Opposite: The interior of the tunnel, following refurbishment between 1995-98, during which most of it was lined with an 8in-thick concrete shell. BRUNEL ENGINE HOUSE

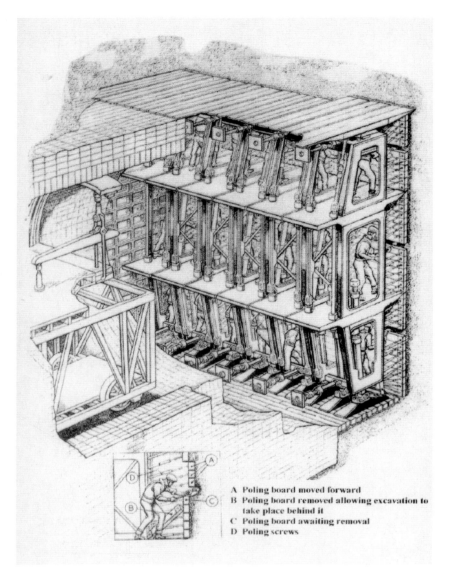

A Poling board moved forward
B Poling board removed allowing excavation to take place behind it
C Poling board awaiting removal
D Poling screws

excavate the earth, and a cylinder supporting the top and sides, until a brick lining could be built.

However, during his time in the debtor's prison, he realised that it could not be implemented with the steam-engine technology available at the time, and so opted for a rectangular shield instead, with all the digging done by hand, in the time-honoured way.

Marc's old ally the Duke of Wellington lent his support for a fresh scheme to burrow beneath the river, and the Thames Tunnel Company was formed in 1824, with Brunel as engineer.

A shaft was sunk at Rotherhithe on 2 March 1825, using a groundbreaking method of building its 42ft-high, 900-ton brick cylinder at ground level and then allowing it to sink under its weight down the hole excavated below.

By July, the shaft had been sunk to a depth of 65ft, allowing the assembly of the shield to take place.

By November, tunnelling towards the Thames had begun, with Marc optimistic that the project would be finished within three years.

Isambard was appointed acting resident engineer on April 1826, and given the job permanently, when he was just 20, on 3 January the following year.

He would stay below ground for 36 hours at a time to supervise the tunnelling, and became ill in the process.

The company directors, eager to make a quick buck, capitalised on the publicity that the project was generating, by allowing paying sightseers inside the first 300ft of the tunnel from February 1827.

The project, however, would not progress as efficiently as Marc predicted. The first of five major floods took place on 18 May 1827, caused by tunnelling too close to the riverbed. Visiting the bottom of the river in a diving bell, as crowds watched from the riverbank, Isambard realised that gravel dredgers had caused the problem.

A 10,000sq ft canvas sheet was ordered by Marc to be placed over the breach, weighed down with chains around its edges, so that 4000 bags of clay could be laid on it to fill the depression, before the floodwaters could be pumped out.

Regardless of the danger, tourists were taken inside the tunnel by punt to inspect the damage as it was being repaired. One miner was drowned when the punt overturned in the flooded workings, becoming the second fatality on the project, the first being when a drunken workman had fallen down a shaft.

The tunnel was cleared of water by November, and Marc was so pleased that he organised a banquet in the tunnel to celebrate. Up to 50 guests sat around a linen-covered table as the tunnel was illuminated by four massive candelabras, as the band of the Coldstream Guards provided musical entertainment. Around 120 miners and bricklayers also attended, and Isambard (Marc was not present) was presented with a pickaxe and shovel.

The miners faced an extremely hazardous and unpleasant task, despite the use of the innovative shield, while assistant engineer Richard Beamish had lost an eye during the work.

Not only was ventilation difficult, and there was the threat of drowning if breaches occurred, but there was the ever-present danger of both poisonous gases and cholera from the foul Thames water. The river at this time was little better than an open sewer, as it was to be many years before Joseph Bazalgette implemented his effluent drainage system for the capital. A fever that caused blindness was rife among the workers and in November 1825, Marc also fell ill.

His son also narrowly escaped death when water burst

into the tunnel again, on 12 January 1828. Having managed to free a timber beam, which trapped his leg, Isambard found that the workmen's stairs were blocked by miners panicking to escape - so he turned and headed for the separate visitors' stairs instead.

A huge wave of water swept through the tunnel, swamping Isambard – but also carrying him to safety at the top of the 42ft Rotherhithe shaft. However, six workmen, including two who had been working with Isambard when the inundation occurred, died.

The flood led the directors to abandon the tunnel, which by then had reached 605ft. Not good news at a time when the country was suffering from an economic slump; the tunnel had drained all the available finances, after 30 times the amount of clay used to repair the first breach had been dumped on the riverbed to allow the workings to be pumped dry again.

Wellington again offered his support; publicly appealing for £200,000 to be subscribed to finish the job, but only £9,600 was raised.

So, in August that year, the tunnel face and shield were bricked up, but the sightseers were still allowed a glimpse inside the workings, by means of a mirror. The *Times* dismissed the project as the 'Great Bore'.

Meanwhile, Isambard's injuries had been far worse than he first thought, and he spent several months convalescing in Brighton, during which time he suffered the first of a series of haemorrhages.

Marc continued to rally support for the tunnel and designed a better shield. He suffered a heart attack in November 1831, but carried on regardless, so determined were he and his son to finish the project.

At last, in December 1835, Wellington and another of Marc's friends in high places, Lord Althorp, approved a loan of £270,000 – and boring restarted on 24 March 1835 – by which time Isambard had become heavily involved elsewhere, on steamship and railway projects.

There were further major breaches of the riverbed on 23 August 1837, 3 November 1837, when a worker sleeping in the shield was drowned, and on 20 March 1838.

On 22 August 1839, the tunnel reached the low-water mark on the Wapping side, and in June the following year, work on sinking a shaft on the north bank began.

For his work on the project, Marc Brunel was knighted by Queen Victoria, on 24 March 1841. However, at the age of 72, the tunnel work had already taken its toll on his health.

Finally, on 16 November 1841, engineer Thomas Page ran excitedly to Marc's house with the news that the tunnel had at last reached the shaft on the north shore.

Finances had been drained to the extent that the proposed spiral road ramps to take traffic into the tunnel could no longer be afforded. Instead, as a result, it would only be accessible to pedestrians by means of winding staircases at either end.

It was like spending your life savings on building a Rolls-Royce, to then only be able to fit a seat for the driver. Without the carriageways and the ability to claim tolls from road traffic, the tunnel would never be profitable.

Sightseers were allowed into the northern shaft for the first time in August 1842, and after Marc suffered a stroke on 7 November, Isambard took over many of his dealings with the company's directors regarding engineering matters.

The completed two-bore tunnel - which has a roof only 14ft below the riverbed and is 1200ft long between

Top: A Yates' watercolour sketch of the top of the Thames Tunnel shaft at Rotherhithe and the engine house next to it, built by Marc Brunel in 1842 and now a scheduled ancient monument. BRUNEL ENGINE HOUSE

Left: The red-brick Brunel Engine House now contains a museum – and offers the public regular tours through the Thames Tunnel by underground trains on the East London Line. Dating from 1842, the building was designed by Marc Brunel to contain the steam engines, which drained the tunnel, and next door stands the top of the Rotherhithe tunnel shaft. The museum contains the sole-surviving, horizontal V, stationary steam engine built by J&G Rennie. ROBIN JONES

Opposite top: A contemporary sketch of Brunel's tunnelling shield.

Opposite bottom: A model of Marc Brunel's revolutionary rectangular tunnelling shield, as displayed in the Brunel Museum at Rotherhithe.

both shafts – was finally opened amid much fanfare on 25 March 1843.

Thames watermen flew black flags from their vessels because they knew that their trade was now at an end.

However, others had paid a much higher price. While the official death toll among workers was only seven, it had been suggested that the 'real' death toll was likely to have exceeded 20 and may even have been closer to 200, taking into account the consequences of work-related illnesses, and illness caused by working in the stifling atmosphere.

Queen Victoria gave the tunnel her seal of approval when, with little warning, she turned up at Wapping by royal barge on 26 July 1843, with her consort Prince Albert, and accompanied by Page (who was standing in for Marc Brunel who was away on business) and company directors, walked the full length of the tunnel from Wapping to Rotherhithe and back.

About 50,000 people walked through the tunnel during the first two days of operation, and more than a million people used it in the first four months. People travelled from far and wide to see what was heralded as a great marvel, and a roaring trade in souvenirs - trinket boxes, whisky flasks and jugs, and paper peep-show models, a distant forerunner of today's hugely popular red, pottery telephone boxes, black cabs and model buses - quickly sprang up.

However, it had its critics, not least of all those who found the 99 steps at each end too much to bear - and who preferred the old ferries. The American novelist, Nathaniel Hawthorne, was less than impressed by his visit and wrote in 1855:

"It consisted of an arched corridor of apparently interminable length, gloomily lighted with jets of gas at regular intervals... there are people who spend their lives there, seldom or never, I presume, seeing any daylight, except perhaps a little in the morning.

"All along the extent of this corridor, in little alcoves, there are stalls of shops, kept principally by women, who, as you approach, are seen through the dusk offering for sale multifarious trumpery. So far as any present use is concerned, the tunnel is an entire failure."

Sadly, the tunnel quickly became the den of prostitutes, pickpockets and ne'er-do-wells in need of a free place to sleep at night. Furthermore, it did not solve the traffic problem of London, as trade and population continued to soar, and it was soon clear that more river crossings would be needed.

After the tunnel was finished, Marc and his wife moved from Rotherhithe to Park Street, a short walk away from Isambard's house in Duke Street.

Marc died on 12 December 1849, and was buried in Kensal Green Cemetery. Sophia moved in with her son, and lived until January 1855.

Three years before his death, Marc was said to have approved of his tunnel being converted for use as a railway. In 1865, it was sold to the East London Railway for £200,000 and tracks were laid through it so that it could carry steam trains between Wapping & Shadwell station and New Cross. The first services ran on 7 December 1869.

The tunnel eventually became part of the electrified underground system, and is still in daily service today.

In 1869, work on building a second tunnel beneath the Thames began – the 1235ft Tower Subway, a 7ft-diameter, iron tube which runs 18ft below the riverbed between Great Tower Hill on the north side of the river, and Tooley Street on the south.

A smaller affair than Brunel's original, it was designed to convey a narrow gauge, cable-hauled railway and opened on 12 April 1870. The single carriage was insufficient to carry the volume of passengers wanting to cross the river, and so the line was closed on 7 December that year with the tunnel converted into a pedestrian subway, reached by 96 steps. Nonetheless, the Tower Subway has staked its claim to being the first purpose-built tube railway tunnel.

It was, however, predated by the Thames Tunnel by 20 years, and it was the Brunels who proved to London that crossing the Thames underneath the river was possible.

Their innovation, improved by the methods used by

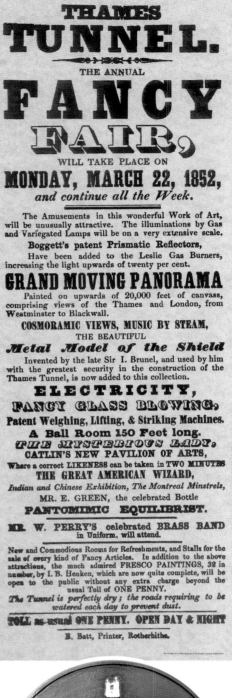

Above: A handbill advertising a fair in the Thames Tunnel. BRUNEL ENGINE HOUSE

Above left: A contemporary, cutaway diagram of the Thames Tunnel. BRUNEL ENGINE HOUSE

Left: The famous banquet held inside the incomplete tunnel in 1827. IRONBRIDGE GORGE MUSEUMS

James Henry Greathead and his cylindrical boring shield (more akin to the circular shield in Brunel's 1818 patent than the rectangular one used for the Thames Tunnel) in building the Tower Subway, laid firm foundations for the London underground railway network, without which London would quickly grind to a standstill.

In turn, the availability of safe, soft-ground tunnelling technology inspired cities throughout the world to build their own underground systems, and even the construction of the Channel Tunnel has roots in Marc Brunel's original shield design.

Many accolades therefore must go to Marc Brunel, his son and the Thames Tunnel. However, the Brunels could – and should – have been beaten by Trevithick a third of a century earlier.

The Cornishman's plan to complete his tunnel by laying cast-iron pipe sections behind cofferdams may not have won the support of his company, but has since been shown to work, and in recent times has been employed in the building of the San Francisco BART (Bay Area Rapid Transit) tunnel and the Detroit river tunnel, for instance.

In later life, after abandoning his railway locomotive ventures, Trevithick sought his fortune in the mines of South America, along with many of his fellow Cornishmen. He did not find it, returned home in poverty, died in Dartford on 22 April 1833, and was buried at a now-unmarked grave in the town's churchyard.

A year later, the Bodmin & Wadebridge Railway became Cornwall's first steam-hauled line. In the decade that followed, a young engineer was to make mind-blowing advances in the field of railways, linking Trevithick's home county to the capital in the process. His name was Isambard Kingdom Brunel.

REACH FOR THE SKY

Bristol and its suspension bridge

xertions with actresses!"
Isambard Brunel's biographers gave that reason as to why he suffered a major relapse during his convalescence in Brighton, where he had gone to recover from the extensive injuries sustained during the aforementioned collapse of the Thames Tunnel.

Whatever the reason, he was despatched first of all to a relative's house in Plymouth and then on to the genteel Bristol area of Clifton, in a bid to accelerate his recuperation. History would never look back.

Once there, Isambard, still just 22, found he was equally as inspired by the sight of the limestone Avon Gorge, as he had been by the ladies of Brighton.

For him, it was a classic case of being in the right place at the right time.

In 1753, William Vick, a local alderman, left £1000 to be invested until such time as it had grown into £10,000 – when it was to be spent on a bridge spanning the gorge.

By 1829, the figure of £8000 had been reached, and a committee was set up not only to raise the remaining £2000 but to hold a competition to find the best design, with a prize of 100 guineas for the winner. And Isambard was right on the doorstep.

He eagerly presented the Clifton Bridge Committee with a choice of four designs, all involving a suspension bridge, with spans varying from 870ft to 916ft – with

both Bristol and London.

Two committees were formed, one in each city, and their first joint meeting of the London & Bristol Railroad was held at the offices of Gibbs & Sons in Lime Street, in the City of London, on 22 August 1833.

When the prospectus was issued shortly afterwards, the name Great Western Railway appeared for the first time.

It was estimated that £3-million would be needed to build the line, but by October that year, only a quarter of it had been raised.

Nonetheless, on 7 September, Isambard was told to start work on the detailed survey, and set off again on his horse.

No railway would receive parliamentary sanction unless half its capital had been subscribed, and so on 23 October, the directors announced that they were to build two railways, one from London to Reading with a branch to Windsor, and the other from Bristol to Bath, in the meantime funds would be raised for them to be joined up at a later date.

In March 1834, the Great Western Railway Bill was passed in the House of Commons by 182 votes to 92, but had then to go to committee stage.

The committee, chaired by Lord Granville Somerset, met on 16 April – and then sat for 57 days to discuss the bill.

Objectors had to be heard one by one. It was claimed that passengers would be "smothered in tunnels" and "necks would be broken," and that the water supply for Windsor Castle would be destroyed. A farmer also expressed fears that his cattle would die if they passed under a railway bridge. The provost of Eton College claimed that the railway would be "dangerous to the morals of the pupils."

Isambard took the witness stand for 11 days, and was praised for his patience and skill in answering questions under cross-examination. Ultimately, the committee

approved the bill and returned it to the Commons.

It was, however, rejected by the House of Lords on 25 July 1834, by 47 votes to 30 – but by then, the scheme had engendered so much public support that victory for the objectors would be short lived.

The company issued a new prospectus in September 1834, this time for a complete trunk railway running via Bath, Chippenham, Wootton Bassett, Swindon, Wantage, Reading, Maidenhead and Slough, to be built for £2,500,000.

The 116-mile route had the distinct advantage over the shorter and more direct alternative between Bradford-on-Avon, Hungerford and Devizes, because it offered access to Oxford, Cheltenham and the Gloucestershire wool trade, with the growing industrial area of the South Wales coalfield just an extension away.

Company secretary Charles Saunders pulled out all the stops to raise the capital, and announced at the end of February 1835 than £2-million had been raised.

Again, the bill was approved by the Commons and went to committee stage, where it was debated for just 40 days this time, facing opposition from the London & Southampton Railway, which proposed a more direct line to Bath.

The committee returned the bill to the Commons after making a series of concessions, including the proviso that the route should be built no nearer to Eton College than three miles.

The bill received royal assent on 31 August 1835 – and work began within a month.

Isambard Kingdom Brunel's greatest hour had come.

Above: The National Railway Museum's replica of Stephenson's *Rocket* and its Liverpool & Manchester Railway train. Although built primarily for the purpose of competing in, and winning, the Rainhill Trials of 1829, *Rocket* did not play a significant part in traffic on what was the world's first inter-city railway. However, it is generally regarded as marking the watershed between early steam locomotives and 'modern' types, which would be used by Isambard Brunel on his Great Western Railway. ROBIN JONES

Left: Isambard Brunel's signature.

BIGGEST IS BEST

Brunel broad gauge

Does anyone remember the early days of commercially affordable video recorders, and the magnificent V2000 system, with its ability in 1984 to offer an incredible 16 hours of play on one tape?

Those 'in the know' considered V2000 to be far superior to Betamax, which in turn was held in much higher regard than the far more commonplace and bulky VHS format.

Sadly, V2000 had been a latecomer, and its promotional strategy never succeeded in elevating it above a third place in the market. It soon disappeared, closely followed by Betamax, leaving VHS to monopolise the home market.

The lesson here was; nothing stands in the way of technological progress, apart from marketing.

As we have seen, Isambard Brunel had ridden on the Liverpool & Manchester Railway and longed for the chance to do better. When the Great Western Railway Bill received royal assent, his big chance came – literally.

The 1834 Bill, which was thrown out by the House of Lords, included a clause stipulating that the new railway should be built to a gauge of 4ft 8½in – gauge being the space between the rails.

That gauge – known today as 'standard gauge' - had been adopted by most of the new passenger-

...nothing stands in the way of technological progress, apart from marketing...

Gloucester, Newton Abbot and Exeter.

As traffic increased and the railway was updated, these one-siders were replaced with conventional stations; Reading was the last to be converted, in 1899.

The section from Reading to Steventon on the Oxford turnpike road, opened on 1 June 1840, allowing a coach connection to the city 10 miles away, until it was superseded by a station at Didcot in 1844 – a case of an early park-and-ride.

Near Steventon station, Isambard ordered a large Tudor house to be built for the line's superintendent; it was also used as the directors' offices and for their board meetings in the early years.

West of Reading, two more splendid Brunel Thames crossings can be seen, the sweeping brick arches of Basildon Bridge, west of Pangbourne and Moulsford Bridge, just before Cholsey.

Furthermore, the short branch from Slough to Windsor includes the bowstring Brunel's Bridge with its 203ft span. It is the oldest surviving example of one of Brunel's wrought-iron bridges.

It was on 20 July 1840 that services extended to Faringdon Road, 63½ miles from Paddington, later renamed Challow. That remained the terminus for five months, and on 17 December 1840, services were extended to Hay Lane, a minor road crossing at the entrance to Studley cutting, four miles from Wootton Bassett. This temporary terminus was later officially named Wootton Bassett Road.

It was from this date that the GWR issued its first proper passenger timetable. Meanwhile, a sleepy little market town called Swindon three miles back up the line was about to be hauled on to the international stage by Brunel and, in particular, Gooch.

Top: Moulsford Bridge crosses the Thames between Reading and Didcot. ROBIN JONES

Above left: This splendid pub sign, at a hostelry of the same name, near Cholsey, recalls *Morning Star*, the second of the Robert Stephenson locomotives, which made the early GWR a success. ROBIN JONES

LET'S BUILD OUR OWN

The rise and fall of Swindon Works

Early in 2006, as plans were being laid across the country to celebrate the 200th anniversary of the birth of Isambard Kingdom Brunel, the frame of a 1934-built GWR steam locomotive, privately preserved 2-8-2T No 7200, was moved out of the railway workshops at Swindon. The movement of this partially restored engine, to the Buckinghamshire Railway Centre, for its rebuilding from scrapyard condition, finally brought to an end 162 years of history, which began in 1843, when Isambard opened his first railway workshops in an obscure market town, with a population of fewer than 2500.

The works were initially built to serve his London to Bristol railway – but evolved into what many described as the finest in the world.

By December 1840, the GWR had reached Swindon; also chosen as the junction for a branch line to Cheltenham and Gloucester, which opened on 31 May 1841.

A station was opened on 17 July 1842 on the present site, built at their own expense by contractors J&C Rigby, in return for the right to operate the refreshment rooms on the ground floor and a hotel on the upper ones, and with the proviso that all trains stop at the station for 10 minutes. This arrangement led to many complaints, so GWR bought back the lease in 1895.

Meanwhile, both Isambard and Daniel Gooch had by then become so concerned about the poor quality of the

locomotives, supplied by outside contractors to run on their broad-gauge system, that they drew up far-reaching plans to build their own.

Furthermore, it was also clear to them that the railway would need a central repair depot for carriage and wagon maintenance.

The pair looked at a greenfield site at Swindon, near the North Wiltshire Canal – this would be essential for bringing in supplies of coal from the Somerset mines for the locomotives, as well as basic building materials. It was decided that this was the right place to build their central workshops.

Also, it those early days, engines had to be changed at Swindon because a different type was needed to pull trains over the gradients to Bristol, rather than the ones used on the relatively easy slopes from London.

GWR directors gave the go-ahead to Gooch's plans

for Swindon Works in February 1841. Work began immediately, with many of the buildings constructed using stone obtained during the excavation of Box Tunnel (see next chapter).

By January 1843, Swindon Works already employed 400 men, including 72 highly skilled engineers - the little market town would never be the same again.

Taking their social responsibilities seriously and determined to avoid the squalid back-to-back houses associated with the new wave of industrial boom towns, the GWR built Swindon Railway Village, a model settlement of terrace houses, which offered far better accommodation than the average labourer or factory worker of the day might expect.

Designed by Matthew Digby Wyatt, at its centre was a Mechanics Institution, where night-school classes for workers and their families were held, turning the

working men of Swindon into well-educated manual workers.

Concerned for the moral and physical welfare of the men under him, Gooch also brought in a works doctor who stayed in free lodgings. A Medical Fund Society was also established – a world first, which would, a century later would become the model for the cradle-to-grave care ideals of the National Health Service.

The Swindon Railway Village community also had a market, three pubs and a church – St Mark's. The entire village was completed before 1850.

The work's first locomotive, a classic 2-2-2 named *Great Western*, emerged in April 1846, and was to become the forerunner of the hugely successful Iron Duke class.

Many more were to follow, and in 1855 production of standard-gauge engines began as the GWR empire absorbed more and more 4ft 8½in gauge lines.

In 1861, a mill to produce rails was set up inside the expanding works, which had by now transformed the sleepy town into a Wiltshire metropolis.

The GWR then decided to build a new carriage and wagon works at Swindon; opened in June 1868, the first coaching stock emerged a year later.

The works entered a new phase in 1902 with the appointment of the brilliant engineer, George Jackson Churchward, as GWR locomotive, carriage and wagon superintendent.

It was his express passenger 4-4-0 No 3440 *City of Truro*, one of a class of 10, which became the first locomotive in the world to lay claim to having run at more than 100mph, at Wellington Bank in Somerset on 9 May 1904.

The works continued to swallow up more greenfield areas, as more revolutionary locomotive types were being batch built, leading in 1920, to the completion of the huge A Shop, which covered 11.25 acres.

By then the works employed more than 14,000 people, expanding even further under Churchward's successors, Charles Benjamin Collett and then Frederick William Hawksworth (1941-1949).

The first GWR Castle class 4-6-0s appeared in 1923, and were followed by the company's all-time flagship, the mighty Kings, the first of which, No 6000 *King George V*, was outshopped in 1927.

The works deservedly enjoyed an international standing as far as engineering excellence was

Above: Terrace houses built for Brunel's workers in Swindon Railway Village. SWINDON BC

Top: The Severn Valley Railway is helping to keep a steam presence inside Brunel's works by loaning GWR 4-6-0 No 4930 *Hagley Hall*, for use as a static exhibit alongside a restaurant, inside the giant modern shopping mall, which now occupies the interior of the complex. ROBIN JONES

Middle: A recreation of a Swindon Works office, inside the STEAM museum. ROBIN JONES

concerned. However, decline set in eventually, but not until Britain's railways were nationalised on January 1, 1948, turning the proudly independent GWR into the Western Region of the state-owned British Transport Commission.

But by 1960, Swindon Works had made history again – by building the last main line steam locomotive for use in this country, British Railways Standard 9F 2-10-0 No 92220, appropriately named *Evening Star*. By then, the workforce had shrunk to just 5000 men, diminishing further in 1980, to just 3800.

As an aside, the fiercely independent thinking of Isambard Brunel as evinced by his designs and use of a non-standard gauge, carried on long after his death, both in the Great Western days and after nationalisation.

For instance, when the British Transport Commission published its Modernisation Plan in 1955 calling for steam to be replaced entirely by diesel and electric traction, the Paddington chiefs stood alone once more.

While the rest of the national network ordered diesel-electric locomotives or planned to electrify lines, the Western Region ordered a string of diesel-hydraulic types.

Just as you could not switch a train from broad to standard gauge, so the Western hydraulics were of limited range – as depots outside the region were not geared up to servicing them – they were limited roughly to the old GWR empire. It was only when the last of the hydraulics were withdrawn in 1977, that Paddington was finally 'brought into line.'

Yet what of Brunel's great works?

Sadly, in the 1980s, when it became part of British Rail Engineering Ltd, the Swindon Works failed to win outside orders, meaning it was only a matter of time before the inevitable happened. On 27 March 1986, this once-great railway town was told the terrible news that Isambard Brunel's works were to close, for good.

That was not the end of the story. Bill Parker, a chartered surveyor and steam enthusiast, successfully set up a charitable trust to keep railway engineering alive in part of the works, repairing and restoring old engines for use on preserved and tourist lines throughout Britain.

Bill eventually moved the operation out of the town to a redundant colliery engine house at Bream, in the Forest of Dean – naming it Swindon Railway Workshops – but a succession of other operators took up the mantle and used the old site for steam engine

repairs on a limited basis.

The final occupant, a group calling itself the GWR Heritage Trust, moved out early in 2006, after its lease on 9 Shop ended, and selling much of the remaining Great Western equipment for re-use in a workshop repairing locomotives and stock for the preserved Churnet Valley Railway in Staffordshire.

Much of the rest of Brunel's works has found a new lease of life as the McArthur Glen Designer Outlet Village, a modern shopping complex, which has at least preserved the fabric of the surviving buildings.

Meanwhile, a Grade II listed, 72,000sq ft Victorian machine shop on the site has been restored as the awardwinning STEAM - Museum of the Great Western Railway, at a cost of £13-million.

Setting out to tell the story of Swindon and the GWR from the days of Brunel, this marvellous museum focuses on the contribution made by ordinary men and their families to the success of Brunel's works and its legacy.

Among the many locomotive exhibits are *King George V*, which in 1971, became the first steam engine allowed back on the national network – after the 1968 steam ban imposed by the British Railways Board – and No 4073 *Caerphilly Castle*, the first Castle to be built.

STEAM, which has interactive displays and takes the visitor through cameo scenes depicting life in the works, and a 'time corridor' of its history – beginning with Brunel – replaced the town's former GWR Museum in Faringdon Road. That had been housed in a hostel built by the GWR in 1854 and which subsequently became a Wesleyan chapel.

To save the Railway Village from demolition much of the freehold was bought by Swindon Borough Council. It has since been renovated and much of its essential Brunel-era character preserved. One of the terrace houses has been bought with public money and restored as a museum piece to show how it would have looked in Isambard's day.

Described in 1845 as 'second to none in the kingdom', Swindon's original station buildings were demolished and replaced by the existing structure.

However, the canal which once supplied the works - the route of which has largely been filled in through the town – is undergoing restoration after a century of closure, as part of a revived Cotswolds Canals network; linking the River Severn to the Bristol Avon and Thames once more. Has the wheel of the transport revolution, which saw railways supersede canals, now turned full circle?

Above: GWR Grange class 4-6-0 No 2931 *Arlington Court*, on the test track inside Swindon Works, a place which was internationally renowned for the standard of its engineering. JOHN STRETTON COLLECTION

BOX AND BEYOND

The GWR line from Swindon to Bath

When the going gets tough, the tough get going. That modern phrase might accurately sum up the predicament facing Isambard as he prepared to complete the western section of the GWR line from London to Bristol.

The first half from Paddington to Swindon has often been nicknamed Brunel's billiard table because of its gentle ruling gradient of 1 in 1320.

However, the remainder to Bristol, running over the hilly terrain of the southern Cotswolds, presented Isambard with his greatest challenge to date.

Work on building the west section of Swindon began in 1837 and from Wootton Bassett; where a huge incline was created, major earthworks were required.

Herein lay the first problem encountered by Isambard. Constant rain during the wet winter of 1839 caused landslips at many of the embankments built from the spoil, which had been excavated from the cuttings built by his army of navvies.

It has been said that there is barely a length of line between Swindon and Bristol where the natural ground was used for the railway, meaning all of Isambard's finest design skills were called into play.

However, his work at Chippenham is a joy to behold, and a must for anyone setting out on a Brunel trail. Next to the wonderful Grade II listed station booking office and entrance, stands an office building, restored by Chippenham Civic Society, and which is believed to have been Isambard's office while he oversaw the building of this section of the route.

The biggest treasure in the town, however, lies in the valley to the south of the station. The 90-yard Cotswold-stone Chippenham Viaduct, otherwise known as the Western Arches is also Grade II listed, and looks very much the same as it did when it was built, despite work to widen it in the early 20th century. It is to be illuminated as part of the Brunel 200 celebrations.

...It was estimated that accidents caused while working in the primitive conditions claimed the lives of up to 100 navvies, with many more maimed...

Leaving Chippenham, the railway runs along an embankment for two miles, and then through a deep cutting leading to the biggest obstacle on the whole line, an outlier of the Cotswolds known as Box Hill, between Corsham and Box. This, the biggest stumbling block of them all, required Isambard to pull off the greatest engineering feat on the whole of the railway in order to pass by.

Box Tunnel became a legend in Isambard's lifetime – and for evermore.

Many of Brunel's contemporaries were aghast at his plans to build a tunnel nearly two miles long to take passenger trains.

Because there was a ruling 1-in-100 gradient, one MP had claimed that if its brakes failed, a train could run out of control through the pitch black, accelerating up to speeds of 120mph and suffocate all those on board in the process. Another argued during a debate in the House of Commons that if the tunnel were built, no one would be brave enough to enter it.

Unruffled in his belief that he knew far better as regards the future direction of transport engineering, Isambard and his resident engineer, William Glennie, began work on digging the tunnel in September 1836.

Above: The fact that Box Tunnel remains in regular use today is a monument to Isambard Kingdom Brunel. ROBIN JONES

Left: The interior of Box Tunnel as illustrated by JC Bourne. Daniel Gooch once said that when one of the two tracks was open and workmen were completing the other one, the whole interior was lit from end to end by their candles. BRUNEL 200

From the outset, as many as 1200 navvies were regularly engaged on the project, aided by a team of 100 horses to take away the spoil, which eventually totalled 247,000 cubic yards.

A ton each of gunpowder and candles was used each week during the tunnel's five-year construction, during which time there were frequent delays caused by flooding, quicksand and layers of hard rock.

Work continued 24 hours a day, with labourers sharing beds in Box and Corsham; as one got out to go to work, another came home and took his place. As was the case with mass gatherings of navvies elsewhere in Britain – navvy being a term for a workmen who built a canal navigation using only a pick and shovel – there were frequent reports of drunkenness and disorder in the locality while the tunnel was being built.

It was estimated that accidents caused while working in the primitive conditions claimed the lives of up to 100 navvies, with many more maimed. In the final push for completion, 4000 workmen and 300 horses were

engaged on the tunnel project.

Daylight was reached in early spring 1841, and the critics who claimed that the excavations from the two ends might never meet were silenced when the side walls lined up within an inch and a half.

The tunnel was completed on 30 June 1841 to the stage where one out of two tracks could be used by trains. Initially, some passengers chose to leave the train before the tunnel and rejoin it the other side, having journeyed round by road.

As the line had by then also been built from Bristol and Bath eastwards, the completion of the tunnel also marked that of the entire route.

Well beyond the predicted schedule, the tunnel was opened at last on 30 June 1841, completing the Great Western Railway main line.

At 9636ft, Box Tunnel was the longest on any railway in Britain, and Isambard spared no expense in adding his distinctive grandiose style, finishing the portals in Bath stone to a classical style, topped with a balustrade.

Despite Isambard's boast to the contrary, it was not the longest tunnel in the country. That honour was held by the 11,451ft-long Sapperton Tunnel on the

Above: Isambard Brunel's drawing office next to Chippenham station. ROBIN JONES

Top rightt: The Cotswold-stone booking hall at Chippenham station. ROBIN JONES

Middle: The arch of St James Bridge and viaduct over the Bristol Avon, looking eastwards, from Bath Spa station. Originally the bridge was faced with Bath stone, but it was largely refaced in brick during the 1920s. ROBIN JONES

Thames & Severn Canal, finished 52 years before, but the fact that its roof has since fallen in, presenting a major hurdle to bids to achieve restoration of through navigation, while Box Tunnel is still in regular use today, weighs any argument about an ability to stand the test of time back in Isambard's favour.

Box Tunnel remains as magnificent today as when it was built, with the First Great Western high-speed trains looking like OO-gauge Hornby models as they pass in and out.

As the railway entered Bath, there was another major hurdle to cross – the first purpose-built route between London and the Roman city, in the form of the Kennet & Avon Canal.

A section of the canal at Sydney Gardens, a Bath pleasure park, needed to be diverted.

Isambard again ripped up the architect's rule book, coming up with a 27ft-high retaining wall, 5ft thick in places, in order to create a barrier between his railway cutting and the canal.

Again, Isambard treated the infrastructure of his railway as if it was a work of art: how many engineers of his day, or even afterwards, managed to so successfully merge the two disciplines, even if he was spending other people's money in the process?

Deliberately enhancing the appearance of the pleasure gardens, next to the retaining wall, he provided a stone and an ornamental cast-iron bridge to link the two parts of the park, which had been bisected by both railway and canal, and added a skewed stone bridge to carry Sydney Road – a much smaller task than Box Tunnel, but a masterpiece nonetheless.

Opposite centre: Brunel's retaining wall and ornamental bridges in Bath's Sydney Gardens. ROBIN JONES

Top: The central span of the limestone Western Arches at Chippenham still look much the same as they did when they were built, although the town-centre side has been covered in brick. ROBIN JONES

Left: A hand-coloured postcard of the eastern end of Box Tunnel, as it looked in the early 20th century.

Top right: Brunel's original skew bridge over the Avon, immediately west of Bath Spa station, long since replaced by a girder bridge. BRUNEL 200

Opposite bottom: The neo-Tudor frontage of Bath Spa station has retained its Brunel design well. ROBIN JONES

Further major engineering work was needed as the railway passed through Regency Bath, where it is carried mainly on embankments and viaducts.

There had been much local opposition to the coming of the railway, and Brunel was called on to work overtime to solve the seemingly impossible puzzle of how his line could serve the city, without damaging the richness of its historic areas.

He decided to follow the canal and Bristol Avon as closely as possible, crossing the river twice, either side of Bath station, with an acutely skewed stone bridge on the Bristol side.

As a result, Bath's 18th-century grandeur was left untouched, with the south side of the city left dominated by railway viaducts and embankments.

Brunel designed the splendid two-storey frontage of Bath Spa station in a Jacobean style.

Its platforms were built on an embankment above street level and the original wooden train shed of 1841 had an overall mock-hammer beam roof with a span of 60ft, while the booking office and other facilities lay in the basement.

Again, no expense appears to have been spared in giving the spa resort a station befitting its popularity with the high-class society of the day, even though there were many residents who would rather not have had a railway at all.

Sadly, the roof was taken off at the end of the 19th century, but nonetheless, Bath Spa station still proudly retains many of the superb features of its Brunel-designed architecture, and richly deserves its place in this magnificent Regency city.

Box Tunnel remains as magnificent today as when it was built...

TEMPLE MEADS
The first great terminus

The relatively short Great Western Railway route between Bath and Bristol proved to be fraught with difficulties. While none of them were on anything like the scale of the task of tunnelling through Box Hill, seven tunnels were needed on this section, in addition to numerous deep cuttings and a two-mile-long embankment near Keynsham, not to mention a 28-arch viaduct at Twerton, as the railway left Bath. Furthermore, a short section of the Bristol Avon needed to be diverted near Fox's Wood Tunnel.

The first contract for building work in Bristol itself was placed in March 1836, but difficulties with the contractor and, yet again, prolonged wet weather, delayed completion by at least a year.

The line between Bristol and Bath opened to the public on 31 August 1840, 10 days after Isambard privately treated some of the directors of the GWR's Bristol committee to the first train trip from there to Bath, behind Firefly class 2-2-2 locomotive *Arrow*. There was no carriage, so the party had to travel on the locomotive footplate.

When this short section of the trunk route officially opened, more than 5000 passengers were carried on the railway on the first day. Neither city ever had cause to look back.

The Brunel transport revolution continued with the building of Bristol's Temple Meads station. Predating his stylish rebuilt Paddington terminus by nearly 15 years, it set new standard for others to follow in its wake.

Building work at the site – which lay a fair walk away from the city centre – began in 1838. The frontage on Temple Gate was designed in Brunel's grandiose neo-Tudor style, with tall square-headed widows and heavy mullions, to screen the engine and train sheds behind it, which were supported by a series of 44 massive brick-flattened arches at 10ft intervals.

A 74ft single-span hammer beam roof, built entirely from wood, in a direct copy of London's Westminster Hall, covered the 220ft-long train shed and its five broad-gauge tracks.

The GWR boardroom and booking hall occupied the first floor of the offices that were linked to the train shed, with the station superintendent living on the top floor, and the company clerk's quarters on the ground floor.

Members of the Bristol committee, possibly disappointed at the very basic facilities originally provided at the Paddington end of the line, had demanded a terminus with architectural features that were in harmony with other buildings in the ancient port, regardless of higher expense.

A letter was sent to the GWR's London committee arguing that Brunel's stylish design could be implemented for just £90 more than a basic building resembling a workhouse – and members agreed.

At the far end of the station were facilities for locomotive servicing and maintenance, with chimneys to take the excess steam and smoke away. The station also had its own goods depot.

The completed Great Western main line was opened on 30 June 1841, when a directors' special left Paddington at 8am and arrived in Bristol four hours later.

By 1845, the timing for an express train between the two cities was reduced to just three hours – light speed at a time when a stagecoach journey from Bath to London could take days, and comparing favourably to

the one hour and 40 minutes taken by today's high-speed trains.

The magnitude of such an achievement can only really be appreciated when you consider the rural and isolated nature of much of Britain at the time. Most towns and village kept their own time, which could vary considerably from that of London. It was only the coming of the railways that allowed standardisation of time across Britain to take place, and eventually facilitated the development of the telegraph system.

The contribution made by railway pioneers like Brunel to the modern world in areas such as this – and so much taken for granted today – was to say the least, immense.

The completion of the GWR opened up all sorts of trade possibilities for Bristolians, who had more reason than ever to be grateful to those Brighton actresses whose 'exertions' had led to Isambard convalescing in Clifton.

Even a decade before, such timings would have been seen as nothing less than a miracle, but now the seeds of the period, known as Railway Mania, had been well and truly sown. Not only had trains as a mode of transport been firmly established, with many of the irrational fears about its effects refuted, but the question now on everyone's lips was – 'how many lines can we build, and how quickly?'

In 1825, there had been just 27 miles of passenger-carrying railway lines in Britain. By 1841, when the GWR opened throughout its 118-mile length, that figure had risen to 1775.

By 1850, it would stand at 6559. Ominously for Brunel and his vision for the future of rail transport, the bulk of that mileage was standard gauge.

In 1845, a second Temple Meads terminus was built, at a right angle to Brunel's first station building, for use by his 'next' line, the Bristol & Exeter Railway, which was also built to broad gauge.

Above: Class 47 diesel No 47484, named after *Isambard Kingdom Brunel*, heads away from the 'second generation' Bristol Temple Meads station in July 1985 .
BRIAN SHARPE

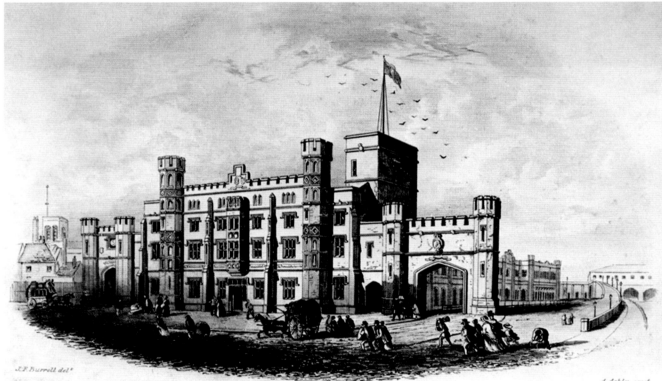

The Exeter line had arrived in 1842, and at first, vehicles had to be transferred between the two railways by means of turntables where the tracks intercepted; moving a complete train one vehicle at a time would take hours.

Eventually, a curve was laid to link the two lines, and it was served by an express platform by through trains.

Top: Brunel's original Temple Meads station is now in use as the British Empire & Commonwealth Museum, an award-winning attraction in its own right, highlighting the rise and fall of the empire and its legacy. The broad-gauge tracks long since disappeared; the station's passenger train shed is now an exhibition hall. One of the themes of the museum is how Brunel became an archetypal Victorian innovator, uniting art and science in his vision for integrated transport. BECM

Above: A contemporary drawing of the exterior of Brunel's original Temple Meads station. BRUNEL 200

The Exeter trains, terminating at Bristol meanwhile, had to reverse into the GWR station until the second station was built.

Congestion worsened when the Midland Railway acquired the Brunel broad-gauge Bristol & Gloucester Railway, for a higher price than the GWR was prepared to pay for it – much to the Paddington empire's eternal regret.

The Midland Railway also gained the right to run its trains into the GWR Temple Meads station, and standard-gauge rails were added when the Gloucester line was converted to 4ft 8½in gauge in 1854.

In 1871, the three companies finally sat around a table and agreed to pay for a new joint station to be built.

The Bristol & Exeter's train shed was knocked down,

and a new station designed by that company's engineer, Francis Fox, was built – right on the curve.

Its distinctive pointed-arched iron roof on lattice ribs was – and still is – 500ft long and 125ft wide. Opened in 1878, it is the stupendous curving Temple Meads that we know today.

Brunel's station original was kept for trains terminating at Bristol, mainly from the Midland line, and Fox doubled its length with a wider and higher pitched light iron roof that joined to the roof of his new station. The two stations came together in a V formation, and Matthew Digby Wyatt designed an entrance building in French Gothic style, to serve both.

More platforms were added in 1935, but outside the curving train shed. However, Rationalisation in 1966,

following the Beeching cuts, left platforms 12-15 taken out of use. Brunel's train shed was closed, along with the rest of the terminal portion of the station and the tracks inside it lifted. The extension built by Fox became a car park, and in 1970 shortened to make way for a new power signal box.

Thankfully, the massive historical importance of the Old Station, as Brunel's terminus has come to be known, led to the building being restored and given a new lease of life as the British Empire & Commonwealth Museum.

It has been said that so much of the face of Bristol today has its roots in Brunel and his works, that it would have been unforgivable if this prize asset, on which Bath Spa station was modelled to a large extent, had been allowed to pass into the history books.

Top left: Ever the showman as well as the architect, the western end of this tunnel at Twerton, near Bath, had to be made to resemble a medieval castle. ROBIN JONES

Above left: Tunnel No 2 on the GWR near Bristol, as illustrated by J C Bourne. BRUNEL 200

As might be expected, as soon as everyone saw the potential benefits from Isambard Brunel's groundbreaking inter-city railway, there were demands for it to be extended to other cities.

When the Great Western Railway Bill received royal assent in 1835, Bristol merchants immediately starting lobbying for it to be extended to Exeter.

Approval for the scheme was granted the following year – and as with the GWR act, the gauge was not stipulated - and Isambard was the clear choice to be appointed engineer.

The first meeting of the Bristol & Exeter Railway Company was held on 2 July 1836. In 1839 it was decided to build the line to Brunel's broad gauge, and lease it to the GWR, which would provide rolling stock and run the services.

The first passengers were 400 invited guests who were carried on a private train from Bristol to Bridgwater in an hour and 45 minutes, behind Firefly class 2-2-2 *Fireball*, on 1 June 1841. The line opened to the public on 14 June, along with its curious branch to Weston-Super-Mare – the first Brunel line to serve a seaside resort.

Because local residents objected strongly to dirty steam engines, horses worked this one-and-a-quarter-mile branch – a real throwback for a steam pioneer like Isambard.

However, the blustery winds of the Bristol Channel often pushed the carriages along or held them back, and in one incident a boy in charge of a horse was reportedly thrown in front of a 'wind-assisted' train and killed.

Steam was eventually allowed into the growing resort, and the branch and its station was superseded in 1884 by the present-day Weston loop line.

Where Brunel succeeded with flying colours at Maidenhead Bridge, he was defeated on the Somerset Levels when he tried to build a crossing over the River Parrett near Bridgwater, with an arch that was even flatter than that of the Thames model – 100ft long, with a rise of just 12ft.

Movement of the foundations caused weakness and the structure, Somerset Bridge, was replaced with a timber version in 1843, which in turn was replaced by a new steel girder bridge in 1904.

Apart from deep cuttings at Ashton and Uphill, the biggest engineering feat was the 1092-yd brick-lined Whiteball Tunnel. The 1-in-81/90 banks leading to it became world famous after future GWR steam icon, *City of Truro* hauled the Ocean Mail Express from Plymouth down it at an unofficial speed of 102.3mph on 9 May 1904, staking its claim to being the first steam engine to have exceeded the magic 100 barrier.

The section from Bridgwater to Taunton opened on 1 July 1842, and the completed 76-mile BER main line was opened throughout to Exeter St David's on 1 May 1844, when Firefly class locomotive *Actaeon* ran the 388 miles from Paddington and back, driven by Gooch himself.

The average speed for the outbound five-hour journey, inclusive of stops was 39mph, and on the way back cut 20 minutes off the scheduled time, averaging 41½mph.

The completion of the BER led to locomotive performances of a magnitude, which, until then had never been seen anywhere in the world. Five-hour Exeter expresses began on 10 March 1845, and when an extra stop was added at Bridgwater, a further five minutes was cut off the journey. What the GWR main line had in grandeur, the flattish BER gained in speed.

Among the 9.50am Exeter-Paddington expresses, which ran between 1847 and 1852, was the fastest train in the world, nicknamed the 'Flying Dutchman', after the racehorse that won the Derby and the St Leger in

THE 'FLYING DUTCHMAN' IS HERE
The Bristol & Exeter Railway

1849. Among engine crews, 'stoking the Dutchman' became a term for hard physical work.

Whereas many Brunel projects exceeded budgets, often because of his grandiose structures, the BER was built for less than the allocated £2-million.

We have already mentioned how the coming of the railway led to standardisation of time across the country; at Exeter, an extra minute hand was added to a clock in Fore Street, in order to show both railway time and Exeter time.

The first rail-borne tourists began to arrive, and among them were an elderly Marc Brunel and his wife, carried there by his son's railway. Tourism by train to Exeter became big business from 1850 onwards, and paved the way for the railway to open up the West Country as Britain's premier home destination for summer holidays.

The BER thrived under the operation of the GWR, who had an offer to buy it in 1845, which it turned down. Four years later however, the GWR lease ran out and BER decided to run its own line, having ordered its own fleet of engines, 10 each from Stothert & Slaughter of Bristol and Longridge & Co from Bedlington, all smaller versions of Gooch's GWR Iron Duke class.

In September 1854, BER erected its own locomotive workshops at Temple Meads, and five years later turned out the first of 23 broad-gauge engines of its own. The works, which also produced 10 standard and two 3ft gauge engines, later became known as Bristol Bath Road, and would become a famous steam depot in the century to come.

Eventually, BER owned 149 engines, with all but 30 being broad gauge.

In its first 30 years, BER paid a very reasonable dividend of 4.5 per cent to shareholders, and opened further branches to Clevedon, Tiverton, Yeovil, Chard, Portishead, Wells via Cheddar, Barnstaple and Minehead.

During 1854-61, the company also leased the Somerset Central Railway, which ran from Burnham to Wells, prior to that concern's amalgamation with the Dorset Central to become the Somerset & Dorset Railway.

In 1867, the BER laid a mixed gauge along the

Above: GWR 4-6-0s No 5051 *Earl Bathurst* and No 7029 *Clun Castle* storm through Tiverton Junction on the Bristol & Exeter main line route on 1 September 1985.
BRIAN SHARPE

Top: Bristol and Exeter Railway 4-2-2 No 10, as GWR No 2009, at Taunton, after having been rebuilt at Bristol in December 1868. It was one of three of these locomotives withdrawn in December 1888, leaving only No 2008 to carry on until December 1889. CW TRUST

Above: The signalbox at Williton on the privately owned West Somerset Railway, is the last Bristol & Exeter one in regular use today. WSR ASSOCIATION

Above right: The best preserved of all the Bristol & Exeter Railway stations is Bridgwater, which is a real architectural gem in this rundown, former port town. It became the terminus of the first section of the BER on 14 June 1841, and the company later built a carriage works and a coke oven in the town. There was also a short branch to the town's docks. The Railway Heritage Trust, established in 1985 by the British Railways Board, to conserve and restore historic buildings on the network, carried out a major renovation of the Grade II listed structure. During the restoration, it was found that the cast-iron balusters of the footbridge staircases were cast by the same firm in Bridgwater that had made the vacuum tubes for Brunel's ill-fated atmospheric South Devon Railway, as described in the next chapter. Sadly, keeping this marvellous building as close to its original condition as possible is hampered on a regular basis by graffiti-daubing vandals. ROBIN JONES

mainline from Highbridge to Bridgwater, in an abortive attempt to freeze out the Somerset & Dorset from the latter town, the standard-gauge line continuing via Yeovil Junction to join the London & South Western Railway.

The original Bristol & Exeter Railway Act allowed for a branch from Bleadon & Uphill station near Weston, to the River Axe below Uphill, but it was never built.

In the 1860s, after the Brunel era, there were plans to turn the Mendip limestone promontory of Brean Down into a major transatlantic port served by the BER, but after a foundation stone was laid on the seabed on Guy Fawkes Night 1864, the buoy to which it had been attached was seen floating off down the Bristol Channel the next day, sucked away by the unforgiving currents, and the vastly over-ambitious scheme was scrapped.

The 24-mile Minehead branch is of special heritage interest in the 21st century, as it is now Britain's longest preserved line, the West Somerset Railway, which carried more than 200,000 passengers in 2005.

Royal assent to build a 14-mile branch from Taunton to Watchet was granted on 17 August 1857 – again with Brunel as engineer and using his broad gauge.

Brunel surveyed the route and work began between Crowcombe and Watchet on 10 April 1859. The line

opened on 31 March 1862, its owner, the West Somerset Railway Co, leasing it to the BER. It was extended to Minehead on 16 July 1874, and was the last new BER-operated route before that company was finally taken over by the GWR.

The lease of the Somerset & Dorset to the Midland Railway and the London & South Western Railway angered both the GWR and the BER, so they joined forces to fight the competition.

Thirty years before, however, a brief alliance of the GWR and BER with the Bristol & Gloucester Railway, prior to its aforementioned purchase by the Midland, discussed pushing further westwards from Exeter, using broad gauge, and on 4 July 1844, the South Devon Railway received its Act of Parliament to build a line to Plymouth.

However, as we shall now see, it was not to be like any main line railway that the world had seen before, and it was to prove one step too far for Isambard Brunel.

Left: A rare survivor from the broad gauge is the side of this Bristol & Exeter Railway coach, turned by horse-drawn vehicle builder, John Perry in Stokes Croft, Bristol. It was 27ft long and had four first-class compartments, with eight seats in each, and a central luggage compartment. It was designed to resemble four road coaches of its day. Now in the Bristol Industrial Museum, on the side of the Floating Harbour, it was condemned in 1884 and recovered in 1966 from South Cerney, Cirencester, where it had become part of a cottage. ROBIN JONES

Top: Many of Brunel's magnificent bridges are landmarks, immediately recognisable around the globe, but, some of his finest works remain in comparative obscurity. One example is Devils Bridge, which spans the Bristol & Exeter route at Bleadon near Weston-Super-Mare. This wonderful flying arch is the highest single-span railway bridge in the country, at 63ft above the trackbed. The span is 110ft. It is thought that the bridge, which today carries single-file motor traffic on Bleadon Hill, is believed to have acquired its nickname from 'Devil' Payne, a local landowner who, apparently, also insisted the BER built him a private station, although refused to stop any trains there. ROBIN JONES

LOCOMOTIVES

Steam behemoths of the broad gauge

Many of the magnificent structures designed and built by Isambard Brunel at the dawn of the railway age, which placed him decades ahead of his contemporaries, have survived the passage of time and are still carrying out their intended functions.

However, even more impressive, at least from a mechanic's point of view, were the steam locomotives that made his Great Western Railway the greatest in the world, but have now all but vanished.

They were truly colossal engines, the like of which we have not seen in regular service for more than a century, similar in concept to, but very different in appearance from, those that many of us remember from the last days of steam on British Railways, or have ridden behind on one of this country's excellent preserved lines.

The Brunel era was the golden age of huge brass domes, stovepipe chimneys, boilers coated with wooden planks and no cab roofs or sides to offer protection to drivers and firemen. With massive over-the-top central driving wheels, the bigger they were, the faster the engine would go.

Isambard's engines were from the days we now regard as pure antiquity, and which we can view only in black-and-white photographs or hand-coloured postcards.

Running on Brunel's 7ft 0¼in broad gauge, these behemoths, with their ability to haul much wider loads at more efficient speeds, gave the appearance of being a completely different type of transport compared to the rest of the country's 'normal' railways.

What's more, they were world-beaters in every sense. Yes, the broad gauge was Brunel's idea, but it was another young upstart engineering genius who 'fixed it for him' – and saved it from becoming a white elephant.

With the appointment of Daniel Gooch as his locomotive superintendent, Isambard quickly proved himself to be a shrewd recruitment manager, as well as an industrial colossus.

Few would have considered an application for a job of such enormous standing and responsibility from a 20 year old. However, Gooch had placed himself in the right place at the right time, and Isambard was spot on when he picked the Northumbrian to be his sidekick, despite his tender years.

It was to be a truly explosive combination, and one that would greatly advance transport and technology within a short space of time.

Isambard may well have devised a railway system, which to him and his supporters was superior to any other, but it was Gooch who provided the means to run it.

Starting work on the nascent Great Western Railway, Gooch was plunged in at the deep end, having not only to sort out the mechanical problems with the motley collection of prototype locomotives Isambard had hurriedly ordered, but also finding out which ones were capable of hauling trains.

Nonetheless, Brunel and Gooch worked successfully

to improve the steaming and reduce the coke consumption of *North Star* when it became clear that the Stephenson engine was not as efficient as it might be.

At first, *North Star* could haul no more than 16 tons at 40mph, but following modifications by made by the pair, which included increasing the size of the blast pipe and ensuring that the exhaust steam was discharged up the middle of the chimney, its performance improved to the point whereby it could haul 40 tons at 40mph – while consuming less than a third of the quantity of coke previously used.

It was through work of this ilk that Gooch honed his skills on the sharpest-possible learning curve and, given a unique opportunity by Isambard, became one of the finest locomotive engineers of the 19th century.

The great disappointment with the locomotives supplied from outside manufacturers spurred Gooch to press the GWR to have its own workshops at Swindon where it could build its own.

He shared Isambard's deep conviction that 7ft 0¼in was the real way forward for railways, because the wider trains were, "safer, swifter, cheaper to run, more comfortable for passengers and more commodious for goods."

Improvement work on North Star and its sister locomotives led to the introduction of Gooch's Firefly class, of which seven different outside manufacturers built 62 examples – in just two years. They had a wheel arrangement of 2-2-2 – the middle '2' refers to the driving wheel – which in this case was 7ft in diameter.

Fire Fly, the first of its class, had been delivered on 12 March 1840 and made its debut on 13 days later, hauling two carriages carrying 40 passengers and a truck from Paddington to Reading.

As previously stated, fellow class member *Fire Ball* worked the first train from Bristol to Bath on 31 August 1840, and Actaeon was used for the opening of the Bristol & Exeter Railway on 1 May 1844.

Gooch also had the honour of driving the first Royal Train, when Queen Victoria travelled on a special from Slough to Paddington on 13 June 1842, behind his locomotive *Phlegethon*.

The fact that he drove both trains highlighted that he was not only a brilliant engineer, but also a hands-on engineman too. Therefore, he could with much justification claim to be the father of the express train.

The Firefly class engines were painted with chocolate-brown frames, green wheels with black tyres, vermillion buffer beams – and a green boiler and firebox. This livery evolved into the famous Brunswick green, which became the trademark of the Swindon empire, right up until the end of steam, and was even adopted by British Railways for many of its locomotives built elsewhere.

In trials between broad and standard gauge locomotives, held in 1845 to determine which system was the superior, Firefly-class engine *Ixion* exceeded 60mph and was able to run from London to Didcot with a 71-ton load at nearly 55mph – clearly far better than anything that 4ft 8½in gauge had to offer. The Gooch engines were more reliable too.

Above: The National Railway Museum's modern-day replica of Daniel Gooch's Iron Duke, on display outside the Royal Albert Hall in London for the GWR 150th Anniversary. This class of locomotive was the flagship of Brunel's Great Western Railway. BRIAN SHARPE

Right: The frontispiece of artist JC Bourne's *History of the Great Western Railway* album of sketches of the line in its early days, published in 1846. It shows a Firefly class locomotive leaving No 1 Tunnel between Bath and Bristol.

Previous page: *Tiger* was one of the world-beating firefly class of locomotives introduced by Daniel Gooch. Built by Sharp. Roberts & Company of Manchester in April 1840 as works number 82. After members of the Firefly class were replaced on the heaviest trains on the GWR by the Iron Duke class, several, including *Tiger*, went to the South Wales Railway. The line remained a stronghold of the Fireflys, and between 1856-65, 17 of them were rebuilt at Swindon works, re-emerging with longer frames and new boilers and fireboxes. *Tiger* is pictured following its rebuild in November 1864, in the locomotive yard at Swindon. Behind *Tiger* is the main office block extension, built in 1869, and today in non-railway use by the National Monuments Record Centre. BROAD GAUGE SOCIETY

THE
GREAT WESTERN RAILWAY.
BY
J.C.BOURNE.

Twelve Fireflys were ferried across the Bristol Channel for use on the new Brunel-designed South Wales Railway in 1850, and they were also employed on the postal service between Paddington and Bristol, introduced on 1 February 1855.

As locomotive design evolved and newer engines with greater capacity were needed to replace them, several Fireflys were rebuilt to soldier on as saddle tanks.

Each of them gave an average of around half a million miles in service, and were so successful that the last one, Ixion, wasn't withdrawn until as late as July 1879.

In 1842, next off the Gooch drawing board were the 21 members of the Sun class, also 2-2-2s, and built by four different outside manufacturers. They were smaller than the Fireflys, with 6ft not 7ft driving wheels, and were less successful, being rebuilt as saddle tanks at the end of the decade, and performing much better in that guise.

Then came the 2-4-0 Leos, of which there were 18.

They were the GWR's first purpose-built goods engines. As traffic levels and loads increased, they too were converted to saddle tanks for lighter duties.

By the time the Hercules class 0-6-0s, the first of this wheel arrangement on the GWR, were delivered in 1842, the company had 136 engines from 11 different makers. Gooch saw that it was inevitable that apart from maintaining them at Swindon Works, which opened the following year, the GWR had to start building its own.

While 0-6-0 goods-locomotive *Premier* (the first of a class of 12) was built at Swindon Works in February 1846, but because the boiler had been supplied from elsewhere, it cannot be said to have been the first locomotive to be completely constructed by the GWR.

As previously mentioned, the 2-2-2 express passenger engine *Great Western* was the first to be built there in its entirety – and what a stunning engine it was.

Finished in April 1846, after just three months, and

visually similar to the Fireflys, its 8ft-driving wheel allowed it to show the true potential of Brunel broad gauge, running 194 miles from Paddington to Exeter in three hours 28 minutes.

The average speed of nearly 57mph was earth shattering as far as an unsuspecting 1840s public was concerned, turning a journey that took several days by stagecoach, into one that could be done in a morning or afternoon.

The locomotive *Great Western* (as well as the company that built it) set new standards of power and speed, taking the steam engineering work of Trevithick and the Stephensons to a breathtaking new plateau.

However, its big initial drawback was the excess weight over the front carrying wheels, which eventually broke its leading axle. Gooch modified his design by extending the frames and converting it into an even more successful 4-2-2.

The first class of engines to be built entirely at Swindon were the Princes, six 2-2-2s all with 7ft-driving wheels, apart from the semi-experimental *Witch* that had a 7ft-6in version, built for passenger work.

While the Princes held the fort on the Paddington-Exeter run for which they had not really been designed, Gooch modified his Great Western design to perfect the class which was to become the broad-gauge flagship, the Iron Dukes, 29 2-2-2s with 8ft-driving wheels.

The GWR broad-gauge classes usually took their name from the first to be built. So, *Iron Duke*, outshopped from Swindon in April 1847, was so called because its trial run took place on 29 April, the Duke of Wellington's birthday. Swindon turned out 22 of the Iron Dukes between then and 1851, while Rothwell and Co at Bolton made another seven in 1854-55.

Above: *North Star* was the engine that made Brunel's broasd gauge really work, but it was not built by the company. It was delivered to Maidenhead by barge on 28 November 1837. This drawing shows it in its original condition. It was later rebuilt with new cylinders, extended wheelbase and a new boiler. It was preserved at Swindon from January 1871 until February 1906 when it was cut up – by none other than a future locomotive-designing genius in the form of William Stanier. Some parts survived and were incorporated in the replica built in 1925, which is now in STEAM – Museum of the Great Western Railway set up in Isambard Brunel's former works at Swindon. BROAD GAUGE SOCIETY

Left: Pearson's amazing 4-2-4Ts gave the Brunel-designed Bristol & Exeter Railway the capability at running of speeds up to 81mph. No 2002 is pictured at Bristol following the takeover of the line by the GWR. GWT COLLECTION

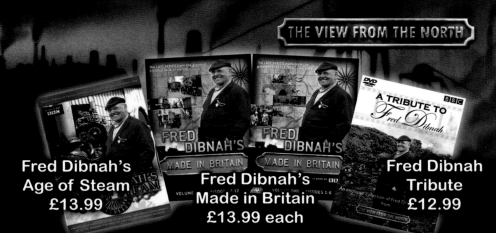

Above: The day before the end of broad gauge, Rover class 2-2-2 *Balaclava* nears Uphill Junction on 19 May 1892 with the 'Flying Dutchman'. Note the Bleadon Hill flying arch bridge in the background (see Bristol & Exeter chapter). GWT COLLECTION

Below: Imagine if, in many centuries to come, all that survived of the world's motorcar industry was a Mini pick-up truck. In the South Devon Railway museum at Buckfastleigh, pride of place goes to *Tiny*, the sole-surviving Brunel broad-gauge engine, in its complete and original form - and it was not even built for his Great Western Railway.
Built by Swan & Co, Plymouth, in 1868, it may well have been the smallest engine ever to run on broad gauge. Running on four coupled wheels, it had a vertical boiler and was designed to replace horse traction on the original South Devon Railway, Sutton Harbour branch, in Plymouth. It later became a shunter in Newton Abbot yard. It was withdrawn in June 1883 and preserved as a static exhibit in the town's railway works. ROBIN JONES

They really were the ultimate land transport of the day. In 1848, one of the class *Great Britain*, maintained average speeds of 67mph on its runs from London to Didcot, and regular timetabled trains were maintaining 60mph – impressive even by standards a century later.

Iron Duke ran up 607,412 miles before it was withdrawn in August 1873, while the highest mileage by a sister locomotive was that of *Lightning*, which reached 816,601 in the 31 years before it was made redundant in 1878.

The most famous engine of the class, the *Lord of the Isles*, one of the stars of the Great Exhibition of 1851, clocked up nearly 800,000 miles in 30 years with its original boiler.

Gooch, like many locomotive engineers who were to follow him, took great care when it came to boiler design, and rightly considered it to be the heart of the locomotive upon which all else depended.

In 1847, the Pyracmon class six of 0-6-0 freight locomotives, slightly bigger than the Premiers appeared, followed in 1851 by the eight Caesar 0-6-0s. However, the largest class of all in terms of locomotive numbers was Gooch's 'Standard Goods', or Ariadne class, with 102 being built at Swindon in the 11 years from 1852. They were so successful that examples survived right up to the end of broad gauge in 1892.

In 1860, the GWR switched from coke to coal as the fuel for its steam locomotives after succeeding with experiments to burn bituminous coal, which Isambard had begun 20 years earlier.

Both the Brunel broad gauge and Great Western empire had, by then, spread way beyond London-Bristol-Exeter.

Gooch had also designed many successful broad-gauge locomotives for the Bristol & Exeter Railway, the Vale of Neath Railway, the South Devon Railway and the Cornwall Railway as well as the Great Western.

To tackle the notorious inclines on the South Devon between Exeter and Plymouth, he came up with the Corsair 4-4-0 saddle tanks, with a leading bogie axle – then a major innovation in design. A variation of these was supplied to the Neath line for tackling the daunting Glyn Neath bank.

While the BER was independent from the GWR, it

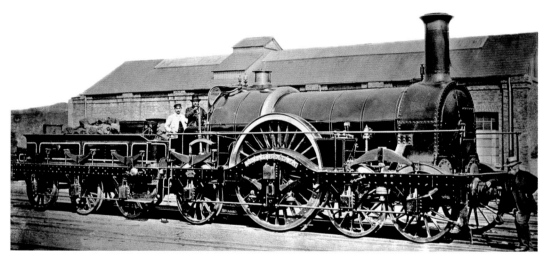

built its own locomotives at Bristol. There, the line's own locomotive superintendent James Pearson, who had worked under Isambard on his initial South Devon scheme as described in the next chapter, designed a type whose spectacular performances easily gave Gooch more than a run for his money.

Rothwell & Co at Bolton built Pearson's incredible 4-2-4 tank engines, with their 9ft-driving wheels, in 1853-54. Numbered 39 to 46, they were used on express trains including the 'Flying Dutchman', and became the fastest of their kind in the country; one reaching 81.8mph while running down the same Wellington bank where *City of Truro* was claimed to have touched 102.3mph in 1904.

In 1855 came the class of 10 Waverleys built by Robert Stephenson & Co in Newcastle. They were the only 4-4-0 tender locomotives to run on the broad gauge, and were mainly allocated to Swindon for working services to South Wales, Gloucester and Bristol.

As well as the BER, GWR slowly took over, or absorbed many other lines, including systems built to standard gauge.

Gooch eventually and reluctantly accepted the fact that the 'superior' 7ft 0¼in gauge system's days were numbered – and set his skills to designing standard-gauge locomotives as well.

His last class designed for the GWR was the Metropolitan 2-4-0 broad-gauge tank engines, of which 22 were built between 1862 and 1864.

These were the only GWR broad gauge engines to have outside cylinders and were designed to work over the Metropolitan Railway, which effectively extended the Brunel empire until 15 March 1869, when the broad-gauge and mixed-gauge running rails were removed from its system. These locomotives were fitted with condensing apparatus to nullify the discharge of steam in the tunnels of what would become an integral part of the future London Underground system.

Its critics eventually brought down the broad gauge system. Yet broad gauge or not, there is little dispute that Gooch's designs had been at the leading edge of locomotive design, and provided the motive power that made Isambard's ever-expanding railway empire work so impressively.

Gooch stood down in September 1864, after years of frustration with the GWR board following a lengthy dip in its financial fortunes.

Top: Rover class 2-2-2 at Paddington with the 'Flying Dutchman' service complete with mail van, 1891. GWT TRUST COLLECTION

Bottom: Bristol & Exeter Railway 4-4-0ST No 48 at Portishead station in 1878. The first coach is still in Bristol & Exeter livery despite the company having been taken over by the GWR. Again, note the similarity of the coaches to horse-drawn road carriages of the period. GW TRUST COLLECTION

In all, a total of 407 broad-gauge and 98 standard-gauge locomotives were built to his designs, around half of them in the new town he had created at Swindon.

While had he begun his distinguished career as Isambard's lieutenant, Gooch ended up with a far bigger fortune and a much greater social standing. A Freemason, he was awarded a baronetcy for his work in laying the first transatlantic cable in 1865 – ironically, as we will see, using a great ship designed by Isambard – a feat which in many circles acquired him greater fame than his railway work.

He served as a Conservative MP for Cricklade from 1865 until 1885 – yet never made a speech in the House of Commons.

Perhaps more importantly, in 1865 he became chairman of the GWR – a position that Isambard had never managed to reach. During his reign, Swindon Works was again expanded, and under his leadership, the GWR recovered from its financial doldrums.

While his locomotive designs were eventually bettered, and broad gauge passed away, in many ways Gooch laid the foundation for the GWR to grow into one of the Big Four railway companies in Britain, after the Grouping of 1923 – and one of the most widely respected around the globe, a byword for class and quality. The *Times* issued daily bulletins on Gooch's health in the days leading up to his death at his luxurious home at Clewer Park, Windsor, in 1889. No other British locomotive engineer would receive such public honour and prestige.

After his death his estate was valued at £750,000 – almost 10 times the amount left by Isambard and equivalent to about £50-million in today's terms. His name lives on in Swindon today in Gooch Street, near the railway line, and the Sir Daniel Arms pub in Fleet Street, which lies near his railway village.

Joseph Armstrong, under whom just 70 more broad-gauge engines would be built, replaced Gooch as locomotive superintendent.

Armstrong's Hawthorn class of 26 2-4-0 tender engines with 6ft-driving wheels, some of which were later converted to saddle tanks, also lasted until the end of the broad-gauge era.

Under Armstrong, the Swindon class of 14 0-6-0 goods engines appeared in 1865-66 and eight years later all were sold to the Bristol & Exeter, returning when the GWR absorbed that company in 1874.

The only side tanks to be built for the GWR broad gauge were the six Sir Watkin class 0-6-0s which appeared at the same time, and were at first also fitted with condensing gear for use on the Metropolitan Railway. Three were sold to the South Devon Railway in 1872, and all six were rebuilt as saddle tanks.

Last of all came the 24 Rover class 4-2-2s, based closely on the Iron Dukes, but having vacuum brakes on both the driving and trailing wheels. Here, it should be mentioned that the Iron Dukes had brakes only on the side of the tender, and none at all on the engine. What would our 21st-century health-and-safety obsessed state have made of that?

Rover, one of three fitted in 1888 with bigger boilers, set the mileage record for the class, clocking up a total of 787,174 between 1871 and 1892.

When, after Isambard's death, it became clear that the broad gauge would become extinct sooner rather than later, GWR had the vision to construct engines which could be converted, if necessary, to run on 4ft 8½in gauge.

A total of 112 were built at Swindon, beginning in late 1878 with 10 Armstrong 0-6-0 saddle tanks. They were nothing less than a standard-gauge design adapted with double frames to run on 7ft 0¼in track, and from hereon, the GWR produced no more exclusive broad-gauge designs.

As the older broad-gauge engines were withdrawn as life expired, they were gradually replaced by 'convertibles'.

Armstrong died in June 1877 and was replaced by his assistant William Dean, who designed and produced 41 convertibles at Swindon, the final batch being 20 0-4-2 passenger saddle tanks which proved somewhat unstable and were afterwards converted into 4-4-0 tender engines.

The steam locomotive now reigned supreme, having replaced the horse as the most effective means of land transport. Yet its dominance was not always assured.

Back in the 1840s, and flying in the face of strong advice from Gooch, Isambard began to wonder whether the steam locomotive really was the be all and end all that the GWR and Bristol & Exeter system had indicated that it was. Forever eager to embrace new ideas, he started looking for the next transport revolution, and saw it beyond the conventional railway.

His vision was, as we shall now see, a main line without any kind of locomotive at all.

Top: One of the less successful GWR broad/standard gauge convertible locomotives was the 3541 class. Originally built as 0-4-2ST in 1888-89 they were rebuilt in 1890-91 as 0-4-4T as shown here. After conversion to standard gauge, they were eventually further rebuilt as 4-4-0 tender locomotives. BROAD GAUGE SOCIETY

Above left: Broad gauge Hawthorn class 2-4-0 *Dewrance* was built by the Avonside Engine Compamy in July 1865 and lasted until May 1892. It is seen attached to a mail van – allocated to Plymouth, it was often used on Ocean Mails to Bristol. BROAD GAUGE SOCIETY

'THE ATMOSPHERIC CAPER'

The South Devon Railway

Sandcastling on Goodrington Sands beach, near Paignton, at the age of five, I was desperate for some water to fill the moat I had built, but my mother stopped me from using the most convenient source, a huge pool which had formed beside the end of a long pipe as it opened out on to the beach.

I was told in no uncertain terms, to stay away from the pipe, as it looked every bit like a sewer.

As it turned out, it was merely a storm water overspill, carrying freshwater from a local stream, to the sea.

Merely? Years after that holiday, that pipe would be 'rediscovered' as an artefact of priceless historical worth.

It was nothing less than the a rare surviving section of the strangest length of main line railway that Britain had ever known – the South Devon Atmospheric Railway – whose designer was none other than Isambard Brunel.

In September 1844, Brunel and Daniel Gooch joined other eminent engineers of the day to witness a demonstration by inventors, Samuel Clegg and Jacob Samuda, of an atmospheric train on the one-and-a-half-mile-long Dalkey & Kingstown Railway, which linked Kingstown Harbour with the Dublin & Dalkey Railway.

Clegg, a gas-lighting pioneer, and Samuda, a marine-engineering expert, had patented the atmospheric system of propulsion on 3 January 1838.

Their method consisted of a cast-iron tube laid between rails and sealed by airtight valves at each end. A piston linked to the bottom of a carriage was pushed past the valve into the tube, and stationary steam engines built on the side of the railway pumped air out of the tube, generating a vacuum ahead of the piston.

The greater pressure of the atmosphere behind the piston would force it along the tube and pull the carriage with it, without the need for a locomotive.

The Brunels' failed experiments with the Gaz Engine over the course of a decade, had done little to dampen Isambard's enthusiasm about finding a better alternative to steam traction, and with the atmospheric system, he believed he had found it at last.

One of the biggest complaints about steam trains – especially in the days of roofless carriages – was that they showered passengers with hot water and cinders.

By contrast, here was the world's first 'green' transport system – clean, silent and fast.

Since there was no engine, the trains would be lighter and more efficient, and the tracks could be built more cheaply.

Hilly terrain could be tackled without having to bring in extra locomotives and crews, for all that would be needed would be another pumping station close by.

The atmospheric system offered all the benefits that electric traction would present in modern times.

Isambard's enthusiasm for the atmospheric system was shared by Prime Minister, Sir Robert Peel, who wanted to see all railways converted to the method.

It may have been logical to assume that just as it had taken 25 years from Trevithick's 1804 pioneer steam engine, to the success of *Rocket* at the Rainhill Trials,

...Here was the world's first 'green' transport system – clean, silent and fast.

Above: A truly atmospheric railway: the pumping station at Dawlish, in a painting by Condy, with the vacuum pipe running between the rails. ELTON COLLECTION, IRONBRIDGE GORGE MUSEUM TRUST

that it would take a similar length of time for atmospheric traction to 'catch on.' After all, it was only in the 1830s that the long-distance steam railway finally proved to be practical in both engineering and financial terms.

In the 'railway mania' of the 1840s, when interest in railway shares reached ridiculous levels, before a spectacular crash, the proposers of atmospheric lines could easily find the financial backing they needed.

After the atmospheric Dublin & Kingstown Railway came the London & Croydon in 1846, eventually running seven-and-a-half miles from Croydon to New Cross in London and the 1.4-mile Paris & St-Germain Railway from Bois de Vezinet to St-Germain in Paris in 1847.

The fourth would be the South Devon Railway.

After completing the successful Bristol & Exeter Railway in 1836, Isambard now looked to take the broad gauge all the way to Penzance. However, his early surveys of possible routes for a continuation of the mainline to Plymouth showed a seemingly endless number of gradients, which could be difficult for steam trains of the day, even if Dartmoor and its foothills were bypassed.

His chosen route would have to tackle inclines at places west of Newton Abbot, such as Hemerdon and Rattery, which were later to become legendary in terms of proving locomotive and crew performances.

As atmospheric traction did not depend on the adhesion of heavy locomotives to the rails, Isambard could economise on earthworks and allow such steep inclines.

He concluded that to boost power on the heavy gradients, with atmospheric propulsion all you had to do would be to increase the diameter of the vacuum pipe, add a second pipe, or just build another, or a bigger pumping station.

Appointed as engineer to the South Devon Railway,

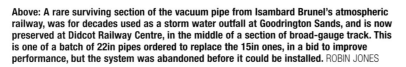

Above: A rare surviving section of the vacuum pipe from Isambard Brunel's atmospheric railway, was for decades used as a storm water outfall at Goodrington Sands, and is now preserved at Didcot Railway Centre, in the middle of a section of broad-gauge track. This is one of a batch of 22in pipes ordered to replace the 15in ones, in a bid to improve performance, but the system was abandoned before it could be installed. ROBIN JONES

Top: A British Rail, blue-liveried Class 45, leaves Dawlish, en route for Exeter, with a service train in summer 1985. This stretch of Isambard Brunel's main line is the most costly in Britain to maintain, not just because of damage by wave action but because of the danger of cliff falls on the far side. In 2004, Network Rail employed contractors to erect safety fencing to protect the line, and mesh to cover the sandstone. The mesh will encourage foliage to cover the trademark, red sandstone cliffs and, sadly, spoil their appearance. BRIAN SHARPE

Right: Preserved Great Western Railway 4-6-0, No 5051 *Earl Bathurst* and No 4930 *Hagley Hall,* storm through Horse Cove tunnel with a Bristol-Plymouth charter on 7 July 1985, during the Great Western Railway 150 celebrations. They did not make it, running out of steam on the South Devon banks, despite doubling up. Brunel foresaw such problems with steam traction on the route a century before, and that is why he opted for the atmospheric system. BRIAN SHARPE

which received its royal assent on 4 July 1844, he recommended adoption of a proposal from Clegg and Samuda to install atmospheric propulsion over the whole length of the 52-mile route from Exeter to Plymouth – even though his trusted locomotive superintendent, Gooch, argued that a locomotive would run the Kingstown line more cheaply, and joined forces with Robert Stephenson to argue the case against the new system.

However, lured by Isambard's promise of huge savings by using the Clegg and Samuda system, the South Devon directors unanimously approved his plan.

In an expression of grandeur, by now inextricably linked with Isambard Brunel's style of architecture, huge Italianate engine houses were built at three-mile intervals along the route from Exeter to Teignmouth, hugging the coast and creating a stunningly picturesque route through a series of tunnels, linking romantic red-sand beaches and coves.

The construction of this section of the line may be viewed either as an engineering marvel or an absurdity. It travelled along the foot of storm-lashed cliffs and nowadays is the most expensive part of the national rail network to maintain because of marine erosion and rock falls, causing regular stoppages and delays.

Isambard was indeed a visionary, but he could not have foreseen global warming and the danger to this stretch of line which may not be presented by rising sea levels. Calls made over the years to find an alternative to the sea wall route – worried about the constant erosion, the GWR itself considered building one slightly inland before World War Two broke out – are now intensifying, amidst fears that closures through storm surges could become a regular occurrence.

Nonetheless, the greenhouse effect was more than a century and a half away when Isambard began taking the air very seriously indeed – but only in the form of atmospheric pressure in a pipe.

Nine lineside steam-pumping houses in all were built, at Exeter St Davids, Countess Wear, Turf Locks, Starcross, Dawlish, Bishopsteignton, Newton Abbot, Totnes, and one at Torre in Torquay, to serve a projected branch line. The last two were never used.

Sadly, the system, dubbed 'the atmospheric caper' by

Above: Brunel's Dawlish sea wall is one of the best-loved sections of mainline railway in Europe. Its storm surges, which send spray crashing over trains, have inspired many generations of top artists, including John Austin of Bridgnorth, who won the Guild of Railway Artists Annual Award, in 2005, for the eighth successive year, with his *King at Dawlish III*.

Right: A sketch of Newton Abbot station in 1848, showing the pumping house. NEWTON ABBOT MUSUEM

Opposite top: Sections of the pictorial survey compiled for the construction of the atmospheric railway. BRUNEL 200

Opposite bottom: Steam successfully replaced the atmospheric system on the South Devon Railway, despite Brunel's reservations about locomotives on the steep South Devon Banks. A 'conventional' broadgauge train storms north from Teignmouth, in a picture taken after 6 July 1884, when that particular section of line was made double track. GREAT WESTERN SOCIETY

locals, was riddled with problems from the outset. Initial tests had shown that the planned 12in vacuum pipe needed to be replaced by one of 15in diameter. As a result, the pumping engines already installed along the route had to run faster than their design speed in order to maintain the vacuum.

Isambard was either inexcusably unaware of – or withheld deliberately from the South Devon directors –

information about the difficulties which were causing the London & Croydon Railway to break down for long periods – and then close for good after just a year in operation.

This first section of the South Devon Railway opened on 30 May 1846 – using steam engines at first, while the vacuum tube and leather and metal valve continued to be laid.

Two public atmospheric trains ran over the line from 13 September 1847, and from 10 January 1848 services were extended to Newton Abbot, with some freight carried.

High speeds were indeed achieved as Isambard had predicted – 68mph with a 28-ton load and 35mph with 100 tons, but the 20-mile journey from Exeter to Newton Abbot, with four stops, took a slow 55 minutes due to one train having to wait for the other to pass, as the route was still single track.

The Brunels were both men of the moment and ahead of their time. With his atmospheric railway, however, Isambard was a step, or two, or three too far ahead – because the basic materials needed to make it a

success had not even been invented.

The hinge of the airtight valve and the ring around the piston were both made of leather, an organic material, which was totally unsuitable for the purpose, as had just been proved to be the case at Croydon.

The solution was to employ a large team of men to continually run a sticky sealant on the valve to make it airtight. The sealant then proved useless after exposure to the air, so a new compound using cod-liver oil and soap was tried, without much success.

This compound, along with natural oils in the leather, was sucked into the vacuum pipe, and the leather dried and cracked in the sun, wind and salty air, as well as infamously being gnawed by rats.

Air leaked into the pipe through the cracks in the leather and so the steam pumps had to work much harder and burn more coal to keep up the pressure in the pipe.

However, there was no other suitable flexible material available in the mid-1800s. Two miles of the valve had to be completely replaced, while Isambard made himself noticeably absent from the line as the problems with the system worsened.

Furthermore, it was found that the vacuum pipes had been cast too roughly and the stationary steam engine pumps kept breaking down.

Isambard had also somewhat stubbornly failed to extend the electric telegraph system on the line to the

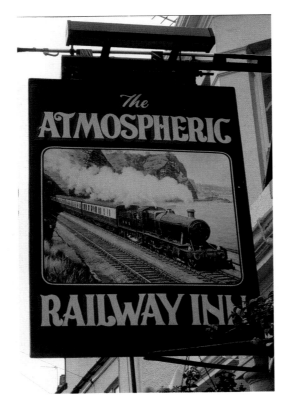

Above: Sections of the pictorial survey compiled for the construction of the atmospheric railway. BRUNEL 200

Right:The name of this pub in Starcross recalls the atmospheric railway, which passes along the seafront, but the train portrayed on the sign is from the standard-gauge era a century later. ROBIN JONES

engine houses. Had he done so, it would have prevented a huge amount of costly and wasteful pumping.

It took a letter from a member of the public to the railway's directors to finally bring their attention to the problem with the leather and the huge weekly expense it entailed.

Calculations showed that it cost 37p to run an atmospheric train for a mile, as opposed to 16p for steam.

In fairness, once teething problems had been overcome, the atmospheric railway showed it could run reasonably well, with nine trains a day running between Exeter and Teignmouth, during spring and summer 1848, when they were reported as having attained average speeds of 64mph. The trains were popular with passengers – apart from those in third class who were asked to get out and push whenever they broke down.

However, alarmed by soaring losses and increasing and unexpectedly vast amounts of extra expenditure, the directors, along with the chairman of the GWR, Charles Russell, demanded explanations from the absent Isambard, and visited him at his house in Duke Street in London.

In turn, Isambard blamed Clegg and Samuda for the failings of their system, although he acknowledged that the pumping stations, which were his responsibility, were not powerful enough.

He admitted that matters would not get better until the pipes and the pumps were improved and completely replaced.

With the South Devon shareholders having lost nearly £500,000 on the scheme, and faced with a £25,000 bill to replace the entire valve after less than a year, the directors voted to turn their line over to locomotive haulage from 10 September 1848, until such time as Clegg and Samuda agreed to repair the airtight valve.

On 29 August, in a rare admission of failure, Isambard faced angry shareholders at a meeting in Plymouth and admitted that he had been wrong about atmospheric propulsion.

He did, however, make one tiny gesture of humility –

waiving his fee for overseeing the construction of the railway until it opened throughout to Plymouth on 2 April 1849 – as a locomotive-hauled concern, complete with those notorious gradients.

The world's other three atmospheric railways were also converted to steam after they too, were scrapped.

The London & Croydon Railway closed in 1847, the Kingstown system shut down in 1854 and the French one in 1860.

Nevertheless, the South Devon Railway, as a steam line, proved hugely successful, and was eventually converted to double track throughout, in stages, in order to handle increasing volumes of traffic. It became part of the GWR on 1 February 1876.

Yet, what if the materials to make the atmospheric system work had been available?

What if the scheme had been better prepared and proven by in-depth trials before the line was built?

Could atmospheric traction have presented a serious competitor to steam haulage, more than a century before the advent of diesel and electric locomotives on the British main line?

Above: The pumping station at Totnes was never used at the atmospheric railway never operated into the town.
NEWTON ABBOT MUSEUM

Top: The Starcross pumping station survives today. Sadly, 'the atmospheric caper' claimed a second financial victim in 1993 when an excellent museum dedicated to this method of propulsion, and housed in this 90ft-tall structure, closed down, following a withdrawal of grant aid. The fine, Italianate, sandstone structure, nicknamed 'the tower' by locals, was sold for use as a boat store.
ROBIN JONES

Left: There is one Brunel atmospheric railway still capable of running in Britain today – a 5in gauge, scale version, built by Barometer World at Merton, North Devon, a firm whose business is based around the concept of air pressure.
The set comprises 100 yards of running track and a South Devon Railway-style train. Staff said that it breaks down, just like the full-size one once did.
BAROMETER WORLD

BRUNEL'S SECOND PADDINGTON
The ultimate Great Western station

Below: The ultimate in quality when it opened in 1854, the Great Western Royal Hotel was fully refurbished in 2001 and reopened as the Hilton Paddington Hotel. Like the station, it too, is of immense historical importance. ROBIN JONES

The phenomenal success of Isambard Brunel's London-to-Bristol railway was such that both termini had to be replaced to cope with greater traffic.

As previously stated, the original scheme included in the Great Western Railway Act of 1835, involved sharing Euston with the London & Birmingham Railway. That was scuppered by a row over land at Camden and Euston, and GWR's movement towards adopting broad gauge.

In July 1837, parliamentary permission was given to build four miles of new line from Acton, to a location next to the Paddington Canal.

The first GWR Paddington station in Bishop's Road was most likely built 'on the cheap' while Isambard awaited sufficient funds to build a far grander design. Its four platforms and plain, wooden-arched, truss-roofed train shed, open to the elements at both sides, was very different from the exquisite terminus he had built at Bristol.

By the late 1840s, the old station was hopelessly outdated, yet the GWR board was reluctant to approve its replacement.

By the end of the railway mania years in 1847, company share values had plummeted. The GWR had to face down angry shareholders in 1849 and tell them that their dividend was being cut from four per cent to two.

However, the directors knew that the station was becoming hopelessly inadequate, and could lose the company business. In late 1850, they changed their minds, and on 21 December, gave Isambard the green light to build a main terminus worthy of both the capital and the GWR. Needless to say, he had already been making preliminary sketches in anticipation of that inevitable decision.

Isambard's design for Paddington, mark two, which was between Praed Street and Eastbourne Terrace, included a train shed 700ft long and 238ft wide, with 10 tracks, five to serve platforms and five to store stock. Consisting of three spectacular, wrought iron, arched, roof spans, it was supported by two rows of cylindrical, cast-iron columns.

Much of Isambard's inspiration for the new terminus was drawn from the 'glasshouse technology' of Joseph Paxton's Crystal Palace, in which the Great Exhibition of 1851 had been held. Brunel's friend, Matthew Digby Wyatt designed the ironwork for the ornate glass screens at the west end of the station, while Paxton's 'patent glazing' was utilised for the roof lights.

The first train departed from the new station on 16 January 1854, when work on the main roof was still being finished. The new arrival side was finally brought into use on 29 May.

On 5 December 1850, the GWR board took on board a suggestion from director George Burke that a luxury

hotel should be built to serve - and complement – the magnificent new terminus.

The completion of the GWR route from Oxford to Birmingham had, for the first time, placed the company in direct competition with the successor to the London & Birmingham Railway – the London & North Western Railway.

The rival company had opened a pair of hotels at Euston in 1839, and the GWR knew only too well that it could not afford to fall behind.

The Great Western Royal Hotel, as it was named, was the first in the capital to be designed as a major architectural statement, and marked a crucial development in the style and opulence of hotel architecture.

Philip Charles Hardwick drew up plans in the French renaissance style of Louis XIV – the huge mansard roof between corner towers creating a chateau-like impression. The building was also the first significant example in Britain, of what became known as the Second Empire style.

The hotel was opened on 8 June 1854 by Prince Albert, husband of Queen Victoria, and his guest the King of Portugal.

Having 112 bedrooms and 15 sitting rooms, plus lounges, public rooms and restaurants, the Great Western Royal Hotel was hailed as the "largest and most sumptuous hotel in England." It set new standards for accommodation in Britain, in terms of size, comfort and amenities for guests.

The design of the second Paddington station served GWR for more than 40 years, justifying Isambard's efforts.

Traffic continued to grow, however, and removing some of the stock sidings and adding extra platforms,

expanded the station's capacity.

While mixed gauge had been rejected at Euston, it became the norm at Paddington in 1861, when the first standard-gauge rails were laid in the station. They served the lines leading to the West Midlands, which had become part of the expanding GWR empire.

Paddington was linked by a footbridge to Bishop's

Top: Paddington station has been altered many times since it was opened in 1854, but the triple-roof span is still an awesome tribute to its designer, Isambard Brunel, and the phenomenal success of the line to Bristol, which necessitated the replacement of the inferior original. ROBIN JONES

Left A commemorative plaque at Paddington honours Brunel.

Road station, which served the Metropolitan Railway's line into the City of London, which opened in 1863.

That line was worked at first by the GWR as broad gauge – and was the easternmost extremity of the 7ft 0¼in gauge empire. However, it was soon taken over entirely by the Metropolitan, with whom the GWR then built the Hammersmith & City line.

Modifications to Isambard's original design have included station offices in 1881, additional departure platforms in 1885, and more arrival platforms in 1893.

Isambard's station needed updating once more in the early 20th century, when the route to the West Country was shortened by the building of 'cut-off' lines, Fishguard Harbour proved to be a major new gateway to Ireland and new powerful locomotives, designed by George Jackson Churchward, all combined to create a phenomenal expansion of traffic.

Brunel's second Paddington station could not cope, and so a new roof span, built from steel instead of wrought iron, was completed in 1915, the year before

---

It is still possible to rediscover major Brunel gems in the 21st century, as proved by English Heritage inspector, Dr Steven Brindle, who stumbled upon Isambard's iron bridge, just as it was about to be demolished in ignorance of its immense historical value.

The bridge, unique and a typically inspired Brunel design, was built in 1838, without bolts, but locking together like a jigsaw.

It crossed the canal next to Paddington station and in 1906 was covered by brickwork and entombed inside Bishop's Bridge Road, one of the most notorious traffic bottlenecks in London.

When its true significance was realised in 2003, Westminster City Council ordered the work to be halted, so the bridge, complete apart from its original decorative iron railings, could be carefully dismantled and stored, pending hopeful re-erection over a nearby arm of the canal, now part of the Grand Union system.

Journalist Jeremy Clarkson, who championed Brunel in the BBC 2004 series *Great Britons*, in which the engineer came second, said: "It is astonishing to think that in a city like London, such an extraordinary part of our industrial past could lie unknown and undiscovered." PHIL MARSH

Above: GWR 4-4-0 No 3440 *City of Truro* stands at Paddington after arrival from Derby in May 1992. BRIAN SHARPE

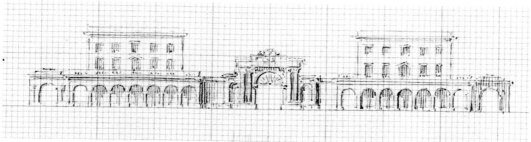

yet more platforms were built.

Further expansion of Paddington took place between the two world wars, with the GWR drawing on government funds to alleviate unemployment during the depression, in order to modernise the station. The platforms were extended and a new concourse provided.

During the remodelling, the once-separate Metropolitan Bishop's Road station lost its separate identity and was absorbed into the main station.

By 1939, Paddington offered some of the finest passenger facilities anywhere in the country.

It took a pounding during WWII, with more than 400 incidents, although thankfully, there was only one major hit, when a 500kg Nazi bomb broke one of the roof ribs in 1944.

Only after the end of steam on British Railways were more major improvements made to Paddington, including, in the late 1980s, the complete restoration of Isambard's triple-span roof, which took several years to complete. Needless to say, it led to a tremendous improvement in its appearance, and thankfully much of the ambience of the 1854 station and its companion hotel can again be appreciated today.

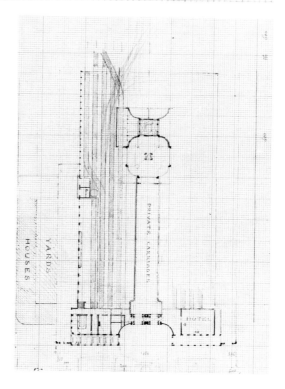

The platform layout at Paddington on Brunel's blueprint. BRUNEL 200

...By 1939, Paddington offered some of the finest passenger facilities anywhere in the country...

BROADENING HORIZONS
Brunel's GWR empire expands

AT one stage, Isambard Brunel had toured the country looking for work. By the 1830s, offers were coming at him from all directions.

Not only had he been placed in charge of turning the Great Western dream into reality, but other new railway companies were also clamouring for his services.

He was given the job of engineer to the Cheltenham & Great Western Union Railway, which held its first meeting in September 1835. He surveyed a route through Stroud and the Chalford Valley, but due to initial opposition – not least of all from the Thames & Severn Canal, the route of which his planned line followed – and the company's inability to raise sufficient finance, the Swindon-Cirencester section was built first.

Leased to the GWR to save buying engines and rolling stock, the new broad gauge railway's Swindon-Cirencester section opened on 31 May 1841. With an eye on a route to the South Wales coalfields, the GWR stumped up the additional capital to finish the route to Cheltenham on 12 May 1845.

Completed at last – but problems were just beginning for Isambard, for at Cheltenham, his line from Swindon met the standard gauge Birmingham & Gloucester Railway. The two companies eventually agreed to share a line between Cheltenham and Gloucester, and a rail was laid between the 7ft 0¼in gauge tracks to allow 4ft 8½in gauge trains to run along them. This was the first example of mixed gauge on a main line.

A simple enough solution? No way, for at Gloucester, what became known as the Battle of the Gauges broke out. On a basic level, this was simply about the inconvenience of both passengers and freight having to switch trains where Brunel's broad gauge ended and standard gauge began, for apart from mixed gauge sections, there could be no through working. The interchange depot at Gloucester never managed to cope in the way that Brunel promised it would; it caused frequent delays of more than five hours and disruption to the transhipment of freight, all of which were seized upon by critics of the broad gauge.

Another company that took on Isambard as engineer was the Bristol & Gloucester Railway, which he persuaded to adopt 7ft 0¼in gauge rather than the originally planned standard gauge. However, this line joined forces with the Birmingham & Gloucester Railway in January 1845, and the pair became the Bristol & Birmingham Railway.

The new joint concern wanted the GWR to extend broad gauge via its route to Birmingham, but talks broke down, and rivals Midland Railway then bought the Bristol & Birmingham.

Not only did it end Isambard's dream of Birmingham to Bristol broad gauge, but left Gloucester as a permanent break of gauge, and in doing so cast doubts on the long-term survival of the 7ft 0¼in system.

In 1844, Isambard surveyed the route for the projected Oxford, Worcester & Wolverhampton Railway and another from Oxford to Rugby via Banbury, both of which were to be broad gauge. The plans meant penetrating deep into the heart of the territory of GWR's rivals – the London & Birmingham Railway, which opposed them and came up with alternative routes of its own.

A panel of five commissioners of the Board of Trade met to decide which of the opposing schemes should be allowed to proceed, and after first taking a stand against broad gauge, eventually supported it.

In early 1845, broad gauge critic Richard Cobden MP, persuaded the House of Commons to consider the need for a uniform gauge across Britain's railway network to be investigated by a Royal Commission.

Isambard gave evidence on 25 October 1845, answering 200 questions, and said that if he had his time all over again, he would still choose broad gauge, despite severe criticism from fellow railway pioneers like Robert Stephenson.

Right: Isambard Brunel's tubular suspension bridge for the South Wales Railway across the River Wye at Chepstow, provided a direct rail link to London. ELTON COLLECTION, IRONBRIDGE GORGE MUSEUMS TRUST

He was also asked why, when he was appointed engineer of the Taff Vale Railway in 1836, as well as taking a key role in the construction of a line from Turin to Genoa in Italy, he had allowed those lines to be built to standard gauge if he was convinced that 7ft 0¼in was superior. He said that in both cases, the higher speeds, which were then a distinct advantage of broad gauge, were not a priority.

Isambard persuaded the commissioners to hold a series of tests to measure the performances of locomotives of both gauges against each other. This event became known as the Gauge Trials, and was a turning point in British railway history.

As previously mentioned, a Daniel Gooch Firefly 2-2-2, *Ixion*, easily outperformed a Stephenson 'long boiler' standard-gauge engine, No 54, which even derailed during one test run.

The commissioners retired to consider their verdict, which they delivered in 1846.

They acknowledged that Brunel's gauge was superior to 4ft 8½in, in terms of speed, safety and passenger convenience, and praised the design of his railways.

However, they said these factors mattered less than the general commercial traffic needs of the country, and in terms of nationwide freight shipment, standard gauge was better.

Could their verdict have been anything but biased against hard facts as presented by Isambard? At the time of the trials, there were just 274 miles of broad-gauge railway, but 1901 of standard gauge. It was so much more convenient and cost effective to let VHS win the day, and sound the death knell for V2000. Needless to say, Isambard was furious.

In July 1846, Parliament passed 'an Act for the Regulating of Railways', stipulating the new lines should be standard gauge, except where any future Act empowering a particular line gave special powers to choose a different width between the rails.

The short and medium-term message to Isambard was simple: carry on building broad gauge. But in the longer term…

He then turned his attention to the 90-mile Oxford, Worcester & Wolverhampton Railway, which now had the green light as a broad-gauge route.

The construction of this route became fraught with difficulties; not least of all the company's financial difficulties, but more spectacularly, an incident, which became known as the Battle of Mickleton Tunnel.

During the boring of the tunnel beneath the Cotswold Hills, near Chipping Campden, Isambard became involved in a dispute with the contractors, Robert Mudge-Marchant, over payment.

Despite being warned by magistrates that he would be causing a breach of the peace, on 17 July 1851, Brunel arrived at the tunnel site with an army of navvies to evict the contractor – the Riot Act had to be read to ensure peace.

Brunel was back the next day with more navvies, and a series of fights broke out, though not on the scale that the authorities had feared. He won the day, and forced the contractor to reach a settlement.

However, during a national recession, funds for building the line fell short, leaving shareholders angry at GWR's failure to invest sufficient capital to make up the shortfall. Eventually, it was opened in stages – but as a standard-gauge line, and with help from GWR's rivals the Midland Railway and the London & North Western Railway. After several legal battles, in 1858 GWR gave up its insistence that a broad-gauge rail be laid on the route; five years later it became absorbed into the Paddington empire as the West Midland Railway.

By 1858, the Old Worse and Worse (the Oxford, Worcester and Wolverhampton) as it was known, may not have mattered, for GWR broad-gauge trains were by then able to run to Birmingham by a more direct route from Paddington. A mixed-gauge line, authorised in 1846 as the Birmingham & Oxford Junction Railway, opened in 1852, placing it in direct competition with the London & North Western, which by then included the route of the London & Birmingham Railway from Euston.

The GWR's successful march to Birmingham began on 12 June 1844 when it opened a 12-mile branch from Didcot to Oxford, having amalgamated with the scheme's promoter, the Oxford Railway, 33 days previously.

The Oxford & Rugby Railway was promoted at a public meeting on 18 May 1844, attended by several top GWR officials, including Isambard. He argued in vain that the line should first be built to Birmingham, not Rugby.

The Oxford & Rugby received its enabling Act of Parliament the following year, and work started on 4 August 1845.

The Rugby option was eventually discarded in an attempt to reduce opposition from rival companies to GWR schemes elsewhere, and so the line proceeded north to Banbury, to which trains first ran on 2 September 1850, reaching Fenny Compton on 1 October 1852.

A scheme to build a Birmingham & Oxford Junction Railway and associated lines to Wolverhampton and Dudley received Royal Assent on 3 August 1846, but legal wrangling meant that it would be two years before final approval was given for the work to start under the GWR, which had acquired these concerns. The same empowering Act also allowed the GWR to lay broad-gauge rails as well as standard gauge on these lines.

In Birmingham, the station was earmarked for a site at Snow Hill, being reached from the edge of the city centre at Moor Street by way of a deep cutting, which was then covered over to form Snow Hill tunnel, with the land on top sold for development. At first a basic wooden shed was provided as a station, before it was taken down and re-erected at Didcot as a humble carriage depot. A much bigger replacement was built in 1871.

The Birmingham & Oxford also opened to passengers on 1 October 1852, the day after a directors' special had been run over the 129 miles from Paddington, behind Daniel Gooch's *Lord of the Isles* – then just three months old, and fresh from the Great Exhibition.

By the time the train reached Aynho, it was half an hour late. As a result, the crew of a mixed-goods train who were uncoupling wagons were unaware of its approach.

The crew finally heard the special, and the driver tried to pull away, but snapped a coupling and left all of his carriages and wagons behind. A collision was inevitable, the special was derailed, but nobody was seriously injured, and the directors completed their journey the following day.

The first Paddington-Birmingham expresses were scheduled to complete the 120-mile journey at an average speed of 47mph.

The broad gauge was subsequently extended from Birmingham to Wolverhampton, but no further. Wolverhampton remained its northernmost extremity, dashing Isambard's ambitions to extend to Holyhead and run an Irish Mail service.

He would, however, reach Ireland another way. On 4 August 1845, the South Wales Railway was approved by Parliament, and guess who was appointed engineer?

Plans to continue the Cheltenham & Great Western Union Railway from Gloucester to Fishguard via Chepstow were scuppered as it was refused permission to build a bridge across the tidal River Severn between Frampton-on-Severn and Awre because of Admiralty concerns about ships needing to pass beneath.

Work began in 1848, concentrating, because of financial restraints, on the 75-mile Swansea-Chepstow section, which included a 742-yard tunnel at Newport and huge timber viaducts at Landore (1760ft) and Newport. This section opened on 18 June 1850, with GWR operating the line, built to broad gauge and detached from the rest of the system.

It did, however, link up with the aforementioned 24-mile Taff Vale Railway, which had opened in 21 April 1841, and resisted attempts to convert it to broad gauge, although a mixed-gauge link line was built from the South Wales Railway's Cardiff station to the Taff Vale at Bute Road.

The GWR then gained approval for a nominally independent Gloucester & Dean Forest Railway to link the South Wales Railway to the Cheltenham & Great Western Union Railway. This line, leased to the GWR, opened on 19 September 1851, but a bridge over the River Wye at Chepstow was needed to link it to the South Wales Railway.

Isambard provided a magnificent structure at a cost of £77,000. Its main 300ft span from a 100ft-high limestone cliff, supported by a 9ft-diameter overhead semi-circular tube girder and cast-iron columns, filled with concrete and sunk in the bed of the river, was followed by three further 100ft spans, all of which stood at 50ft above the high-tide level.

It was a new type of bridge construction, a bespoke solution for a unique location, which typified Isambard's genius and also ended up being a trial run for one of his greatest engineering feats, the Royal Albert Bridge at Saltash, as we shall see.

Trains were able to run from Gloucester to Swansea for the first time on 18 April 1853. It brought Swansea to within six hours of London; the previous best was 15 hours, using stagecoach, a ferry and GWR from Bristol. The line, which used Gooch Firefly locomotives at the start, was extended from Landore near Swansea to Carmarthen on 11 October 1852, with a 789-yard tunnel at Cockett.

In 1844, Isambard had informed the Dublin & Kingstown Railway, the first in Ireland, of his intention to build a broad-gauge line to Fishguard and start a new sea route to Rosslare. His suggestion to help the DKR build a line to Wexford, led to the formation of the Waterford, Wexford, Wicklow & Dublin Railway, work finally beginning on the line from Dublin to Wicklow in August 1847.

By 10 July 1854, the line to Bray was opened. However, serious engineering problems were encountered on the line at Bray Head to the south, where the topography proved difficult for the building of a railway. The coastal route had been chosen because it offered spectacular scenery, unlike the more straightforward route inland.

Isambard used his experience from Thames Tunnel days to chisel through the hard rock and build three tunnels to carry the line, which reached Wicklow Town in 1855.

In Wales, Brunel never did reach Fishguard with his broad gauge and instead looked at the west coast of Pembrokeshire for an Irish terminal.

Pressing on, Haverfordwest was reached by the South Wales Railway on 2 January 1854, and Neyland – subsequently renamed Milford Haven and then New Milford – on 1 July 1857.

In the meantime, GWR helped other schemes to intensify the broad-gauge links to South Wales. The Hereford, Ross & Gloucester Railway linked with the Cheltenham & Great Western Union Railway at Grange Court at one end, and the standard gauge Shrewsbury & Hereford Railway at the other.

Several broad-gauge routes appeared in the Forest of

Top: The sole-surviving building from the Isambard Brunel era at Briton Ferry Dock is this tower at the entrance. Local authorities have now assembled a funding package to investigate the possibility of restoring the dock.

Middle: As well as the magnificent viaducts in the Chalford Valley, Isambard Brunel also built Stroud station, which includes his office dating from 1845, now Grade II listed, and the nearby goods shed, which is afforded similar protection. The Stroud Brunel Group wants to renovate this structure, thought to be the last remaining Brunel-designed goods shed in existence, and turn it into an exhibition. It will also be a focal point of activities to mark the 200th anniversary of his birth in 2006, culminating in the Stroud Country Show on 15 July. STROUD BRUNEL GROUP

Bottom: The extraordinary Jackdaw Bridge in the Golden Valley near Stroud, was built by Brunel in 1845 as an means of carrying an inclined plane over his Cheltenham & Great Western Union Railway. The plane lowered stone from Jackdaw Quarry over the railway and on to barges on the Thames & Severn Canal below. STROUD BRUNEL GROUP

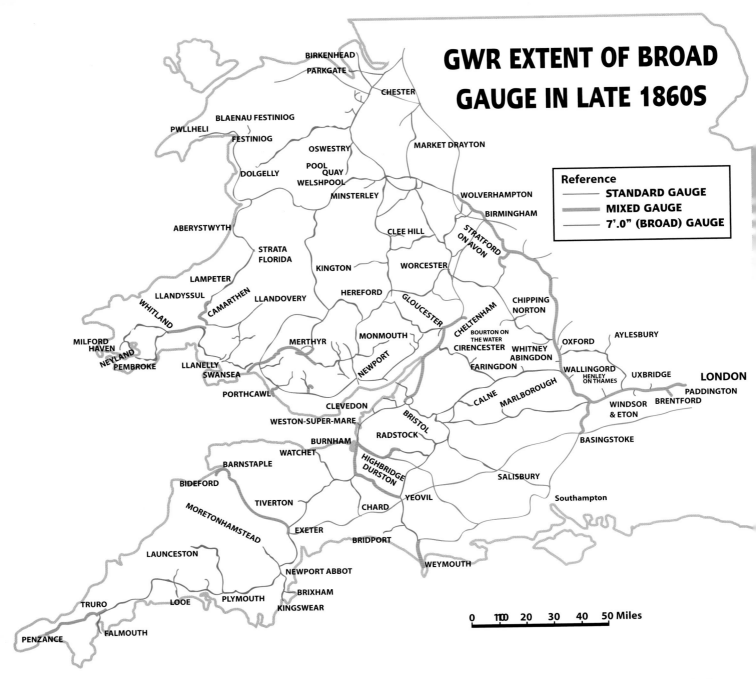

Reference
— STANDARD GAUGE
▬ MIXED GAUGE
— 7'.0" (BROAD) GAUGE

0 10 20 30 40 50 Miles

Dean – then a hive of heavy industry because of its coal reserves. They included the Forest of Dean Railway, linking Cinderford to Bullo Cross on the Cheltenham & Great Western Union Railway, the horse-worked Severn & Wye Railway from Coleford to Lydney, the short Forest of Dean Central Railway from Brimspill to the Howbeach Valley.

Isambard was never short of work in South Wales. He engineered the broad-gauge Vale of Neath Railway, which opened between Neath and Aberdare on 24 September 1851, extending from Aberdare to Gelli Tarw, the junction for Merthyr Tydfil, on 2 November 1853. Excelling himself again, Isambard oversaw the construction of a 2495-yard tunnel at Merthyr, plus major viaducts at Merthyr and Werfa.

He also engineered the freight-only South Wales Mineral Railway, which ran from Briton Ferry along the Afan Valley to Glyncorrwg, and not only had 1-in-22 gradients and a 1109-yard tunnel at Glfylchi, but an ingenious rope-worked incline.

Isambard was engaged in 1851 to design and build a Bristol-style floating dock at Briton Ferry for the shipment of coal, and diverted the River Neath in order to provide a site for it. He built a half-mile broad-gauge

extension to the Vale of Neath Railway to serve a wharf at Briton Ferry, opening in 1852, nine years before the dock was completed.

In the far west of Wales, the broad gauge pushed on, part of the Carmarthen Railway being built to 7ft 0¼in gauge for seven miles between Carmarthen and Convil (much of this section is now preserved as the Gwili Railway) and opening on 1 July 1860. Also, the four-mile Milford Railway, which ran between the South Wales Railway at Johnston and Milford Haven docks, was opened on 7 September 1873 and operated by the GWR.

The broad gauge in South Wales, however, did not work to the advantage of the GWR, which had more than a finger in the pie of all the railway schemes in the region that had adopted 7ft 0¼in.

The booming South Wales coalfield became a labyrinth of independent lines, mainly standard gauge, for conveying coal to docks. Because transhipment to broad-gauge wagons would incur extra labour costs and delays, it was not a preferred option, and comparatively little coal was conveyed on the Brunel system. Meanwhile, rival standard-gauge companies like the Midland Railway and London & North Western began

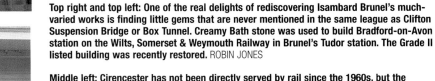

Top right and top left: One of the real delights of rediscovering Isambard Brunel's much-varied works is finding little gems that are never mentioned in the same league as Clifton Suspension Bridge or Box Tunnel. Creamy Bath stone was used to build Bradford-on-Avon station on the Wilts, Somerset & Weymouth Railway in Brunel's Tudor station. The Grade II listed building was recently restored. ROBIN JONES

Middle left: Cirencester has not been directly served by rail since the 1960s, but the station building still survives in the town centre, with a plaque to remind passers-by that it was built by Isambard Brunel. This line was built as the first stage of the Cheltenham & Great Western Union Railway, but later became a branch line from Kemble. ROBIN JONES

Middle right and bottom right: The all-encompassing train shed was a delightful feature of Isambard Brunel's railways, but the sole survivor on the national network is this splendid Grade II listed example at Frome, designed by JR Hannaford and still in daily use. Timber was used for economy. ROBIN JONES

Left: The front of Frome's wooden trainshed, a Brunel building made of cheaper materials than stone, but which has stood the test of time. ROBIN JONES

extending into the region.

The GWR had to react to market pressures, in short, by the end of 1872, the entire route from Gloucester to Milford Haven had been converted to standard gauge, with the adjacent broad-gauge lines following suit.

In the meantime, GWR had also been expanding its interests in the south of England, either directly promoting new lines, or investing in and influencing them as independent but 'satellite' concerns.

The mid-1840s Railway Mania saw the 39-mile Berks & Hants Railway built, under Isambard's auspices from the GWR main line at Reading to Hungerford via Newbury, opening on 21 December 1847, and from Southcote Junction to Basingstoke, opening on 1 November 1848.

Simultaneously, the Wilts, Somerset & Weymouth Railway, leaving Isambard's original GWR main line at Thingley Junction near Chippenham, was opened in stages from 5 September 1848 to 20 January 1857, running via Yeovil and Dorchester. It had branches from Warminster to Salisbury and from Frome to Radstock, (the latter currently the subject of a protracted and stalled preservation scheme), and an offshoot, the Bridport Railway, from Maiden Newton to Bridport, opened on 12 November 1857, and eventually carrying on (after conversion to standard gauge) to West Bay.

The Somerset Central Railway between Highbridge and Glastonbury, engineered not by Brunel but by Charles Hutton Gregory, was opened on 17 August 1854 as a broad-gauge line worked by the Bristol & Exeter Railway, quickly extending to Wells and Burnham-on-Sea, but much to the anger of the GWR, was converted to mixed gauge after 1861 when the operator's lease expired. This line linked up with the standard-gauge Dorset Central Railway to form, on 1 September 1862, the Somerset & Dorset Railway.

The East Somerset Railway today is a preserved line based at Cranmore, near Shepton Mallet. It is, however, part of a much longer route opened from Witham on the Wilts, Somerset & Weymouth Railway to Shepton Mallet on 9 November 1858 as broad gauge, extending to Wells in 1862 and linking to the Bristol & Exeter's Cheddar branch. The East Somerset was

Right: No 2123 *Pluto* was a South Devon Railway 4-4-0ST built by the Avonside Engine Company in October 1866. Atmospheric era aside, the South Devon had originally been worked by contractors and it was only in 1866 that the company started running its own services. This was one of the first batch of eight locomotives delivered to the company that year, six 4-4-0STs for passenger trains and two 0-6-0STs for goods workings. *Pluto* was one of the four passenger locomotives of this class that lasted until the end of the broad gauge in May 1892. It is seen here on an Up working double-heading a GWR Rover class 4-2-2. Broad gauge open and tilt wagons, both with tarpaulins, stand in the siding beyond.

bought by the GWR in 1874.

The Exeter & Crediton Railway was built to broad gauge as it linked to the Bristol & Exeter, but when it was finished in 1847, the London & South Western Railway used its majority shareholding to insist it was converted to standard gauge. The Government's Railway Commission ruled that was illegal, and the line was then leased to the BER. It connected to the North Devon Railway to Barnstaple, which was also broad gauge.

Following complaints that the BER was not managing the line properly, it was leased to the LSWR, which promptly installed mixed-gauge rails, and broad-gauge operations north of Crediton, where the Brunel station office survives today, ceased after 1877.

Meanwhile, another broad-gauge line reached Barnstaple in the form of the Devon & Somerset Railway from Taunton, which was worked by the BER but was not formally taken over by the GWR until 1901.

There were other smaller concerns. In 1857, Royal

Assent was given for the broad gauge Dartmouth & Torbay Railway, with Isambard as engineer. Opening at the beginning of August it effectively extended the South Devon Railway, which operated the line, from its Torquay station at Torre to Kingswear, opposite Dartmouth, which was reached by means of a floating bridge or road-vehicle ferry, as it still is today. A typical station booking office building at Dartmouth was opened in 1889 – but it has never been physically served by trains, and as such acquired a unique status on the national network. It survives today on the waterfront as a cafe.

In 1862, an Act of Parliament passed for the construction of a broad-gauge branch line from Moretonhampstead to Newton Abbot, the route opening as the Moretonhampstead & South Devon Railway on 26 June 1862. The line was absorbed in 1872 by the South Devon Railway which in turn became part of the GWR empire.

It was not the last broad-gauge line to be built, but by then the writing for the 7ft 0¼in gauge was on the wall.

Above: A broad gauge train crossing a typical Brunel trestle viaduct of the type which were commonplace on his lines in Cornwall, South Devon and South Wales and allowed railways to be built across hilly terrain at affordable cost. The frequent use of such 'cheaper' structures greatly facilitated the expansion of the broad gauge empire. ELTON COLLECTION: IRONBRIDGE GORGE MUSEUM TRUST

Top: Torre station, pictured in 1870, was the place where the South Devon Railway's Torquay branch net the Torbay & Dartmouth Railway, also engineered by Isambard Brunel, part of which today operates regular Great Western steam as the Paignton & Dartmouth Steam Railway. The passenger locomotive in the picture is Avonside Engine company 4-4-0 *Zebra*, which became GWR No 2127. Torre remains an excellent example of a Brunel station, but Isambard surveyed more than just railways at Torbay. He bought 136 acres of land at Watcombe and designed a house in which he wanted to live with his family, surrounded by landscape gardens and an arboretum, but he completed only the foundations before he died. The completed Brunel Manor House is now run by the Woodlands House of Prayer Trust as a Christian holiday and conference centre. BROAD GAUGE SOCIETY

Middle: Exeter St David's was not only the terminus of the Bristol & Exeter Railway, but the gateway to Brunel's expanding west of England empire. GWR 4-2-2 *Emperor* stands at Exeter in 1889. GW TRUST COLLECTION

Right: Firefly class 2-2-2 *Load Star* and its express train came unstuck at Carmarthen while hauling the 9.15am from Haverfordwest on 8 January 1855. GW TRUST

Did Brunel ever think that, in the face of opposition from the likes of leading authorities like Stephenson, his broad gauge, while superior in so many respects, would ever be adopted as the norm throughout Britain, or did he envisage a super-efficient regional service serving just part of it, with passengers and goods being switched to the smaller trains of other companies wherever the 'break of gauge occurred'?

Had his system 'got in first', and had been adopted by main line railways everywhere, how different would our national transport network be today.

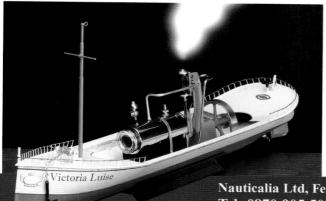

Go Great Western – to New York

THE FIRST TRANSATLANTIC LINERS

While the new breed of steam-railway magnates was busy carving up Britain, the eyes of Isambard Brunel were already set on a far greater goal.

He wanted to extend his Great Western Railway from London, beyond Bristol – all the way to the United States.

At one stage in his career, Brunel had been touring the country touting for work. Soon, there would come a day when he would become the ultimate workaholic – tackling not one, but several world-beating projects back-to-back.

While he was overseeing the building of the GWR, a project that in itself would have placed him among the greatest engineers of all time; he was busy working on a new and very different project of monumental proportions – the world's first transatlantic liners.

Shipping was the last major area to benefit from the massive strides in transport technology, which had been spawned by the Industrial Revolution, and in the 1830s, still owed more to traditional building techniques than the application of modern science.

Just as railways had been the preserve of horsepower until the Rainhill Trials of 1829, so shipping had been based on developments of sail power, with the industry slow to take up the new steam technology.

What Richard Trevithick was to steam-powered road and rail locomotives, William Symington was to steamboats.

Symington was born in Leadhills, Lanarkshire, in 1764, the son of a mechanic who worked the local lead mines, and like Trevithick, became a pioneer in steam mining technology.

Having worked on perfecting one of James Watt's stationary steam engines, Symington was approached by Patrick Miller, banker and shareholder in Carron Company, Scotland's premier engineering firm, to fit a steam engine inside a pleasure boat for small-scale trials. The aim of this early experiment was to demonstrate that an engine could work on the unstable foundation of a boat, and would not set it on fire.

The engine had already been demonstrated on a model steam carriage, which Symington had built in 1785. The partly successful trial took place on the loch next to Miller's house at Dalswinton, near Dumfries, on 14 October 1788.

Miller was so impressed he ordered a larger engine to undergo tests in a paddleboat on the Forth and Clyde Canal on 2 December 1789 and, after several trials, it reached a speed of nearly 7mph.

Thomas, Lord Dundas, governor of the Forth and Clyde Canal Company, looked into the possibility of using steam tugs along the lines of a prototype trialled by Captain John Schank on the Bridgewater Canal, near Manchester in 1799.

He asked for a Symington engine to be added to a Schank-designed boat, which was successfully given a run-out on the River Carron in June 1801, but was ruled unsuitable for the canal. Symington patented a horizontal engine in 1801, which was more powerful, and won the support of Lord Dundas for a second vessel – to be named *Charlotte Dundas*, after one of his daughters – to be built.

It was launched in Glasgow on 4 January 1803 and after some later modifications, towed two loaded vessels along the canal, covering 18½ miles in nine-and-a-quarter hours.

Sadly, the canal company turned it down, because of

fears it would damage the navigation's banks, and it was forced to live out its life in one of the waterway's passing bays.

Symington, like Trevithick, ended his days fraught with financial difficulties, but nonetheless, his *Charlotte Dundas* had staked its claim to being the world's first viable steamship.

The launch in 1812 of Henry Bell's *Comet* on the Clyde – the first steam-operated commercial ferry, was followed two years later by the steamboat *Regent*, plying its trade between London and Margate. Its designer? Marc Brunel, who again showed he was more than up to speed with cutting-edge technology.

The first cross-channel steamship was the 112-ton *Hibernia*, which made it from Holyhead to Dublin in seven hours in 1816. The first oceanic crossing by a steamship was made in 1819 by the *PS Savannah*, built by Francis Fickett, of Corlears Hook, New York; with an engine provided by Stephen Vail of the Speedwell Iron Works, New Jersey.

Originally intended for the sail packet service to Le Havre, it set out from Savannah, Georgia, reaching Liverpool on 20 June, after 29 days 11 hours. However, the engines were sparingly used and for the most part,

the ship relied on its sails.

Up to 1835, steamships were still considered suitable only for short runs in comparatively shallow waters, as the early examples did not have the capacity to carry and burn sufficient coal for anything like a transatlantic voyage.

It was considered by leading authorities, including Marc Brunel, that the consumption of coal by a steam engine would increase in proportion to the size of a ship, and if the existing vessels could not manage to cross an ocean, logic dictated that neither could a larger one.

It needed a genius to rewrite the principles of the 'logic' of the day, someone who had already showed himself capable of doing just that.

Isambard realised that this principle was erroneous, as the energy needed to drive a ship, whether by sail or steam, did not depend on the vessel's weight, but on the weight of the water that it had to shift.

He worked out that the key factors were the surface area of the ship, and its shape, and found that contrary to previous belief, the larger the vessel; the more favourable the crucial energy-to-weight equation would be.

At an early meeting of the GWR board, Isambard was

Above: Standing room only, on another day when Brunel changed the world: Bristol's waterfront was packed out on 19 July 1843, when the *SS Great Britain* was floated for the first time, as seen in this Joseph Walter engraving.

said to have suggested extending the railway by adding a steamboat – to be called the *Great Western*, after the company – and which would go all the way to New York.

One of the directors, Thomas Guppy, did not join in with the ensuing scorn, and persuaded three other board members, Robert Scot, Robert Bright and Thomas Pycroft to set up a committee to look into the possibility. They were joined by naval captain Christopher Claxton, who Brunel had met while working on the improvements to the city docks, and who was able to gain access to official drawings of Admiralty vessels currently under construction.

A low-key prospectus called for the company to build not one, but two, 1200-ton steamships with 400-horsepower engines. Many local people bought shares in the scheme, including Isambard.

A new prospectus was issued before the first meeting of a new Great Western Steamship Company on 3 March 1836, giving further details of the proposed ships and the estimated cost of £35,000 each. Five of the directors were also board members of the GWR.

Isambard roped in Bristol shipbuilder William Patterson to add his weight and expertise to the project. It was inside Patterson's yard at Wapping Wharf, in the Floating Harbour, that the keel of the first ship was laid in June that year, without pomp or ceremony. At 205ft, it was the longest ever to have been laid.

The ship was clearly so huge that sceptics were again at the fore, doubting whether it could ever be brought out of the dock and down the winding mud of the Avon Gorge to the Bristol Channel, let alone set out to sea.

Lambeth manufacturer Maudslay, Son & Field had vast experience in building marine engines and was selected to supply the ship's engines, which had massive cylinders with a 73½in diameter and a stroke of 7ft, and were to drive twin-paddle wheels 28ft in diameter.

The great day came on 19 July 1837, when more than 50,000 onlookers crowded into Bristol's docks and on to adjacent vessels to watch the ship's launch.

As the ship started moving down the shipway, a deafening cry of 'She moves!' soared to the sky, as Claxton smashed a bottle of madeira over the bowsprit.

Mrs Miles, wife of one of the steamship company's directors, named the ship the *Great Western*. Afterwards, 300 invited guests joined the directors for dinner in the ship's main cabin.

On 18 August, the *Great Western* was towed down the Avon estuary by the steam tug *Lion*, and, accompanied by the steam packet *Ben Ledi*, using a four-masted schooner rig to travel to London around the south coast of England as a sailing ship.

The London crowds were equally ecstatic when they glimpsed the *Great Western* for the first time, if only for her sheer size.

In East India Dock at Blackwall, much of the machinery was fitted by Maudslay over an intensive six-month period, and in March 1838, the *Great Western* was moved to a berth in the River Thames for preliminary trials, during which the ship struck another vessel and days later became briefly stuck on a mud bank opposite Trinity Wharf.

However, four days of engine trials saw the *Great Western* comfortably manage an average speed of 11 knots.

Above left: The bow of the *SS Great Britain* in its permanent Bristol home.
MANDY REYNOLDS

Left: The stern of the *SS Great Britain*, as displayed above its 21st-century 'glass sea'.
MANDY REYNOLDS

Right: One of Bristol's real – and mostly overlooked – architectural treasures is the surviving face of what was built as the Royal Western Hotel, designed by RS Pope and Isambard Brunel and finished in 1839. It was intended to provide a luxury stopover for passengers who had arrived in London via his railway, and were to travel onwards to New York by liner. However, it closed down as early as 1855, and the bulk of the building behind the façade was later demolished to make way for modern offices, which now house a city council department. ROBIN JONES

Below: The Floating Harbour with the Avon Gorge and Isambard Brunel's Clifton Suspension Bridge in the background. Two ships he designed and which were destined to change the world left Bristol through here. BRUNEL 200

Isambard had again silenced his critics, including a Dr Dionysius Lardner, who had publicly proclaimed in 1835 that transatlantic steamship travel was all but impossible, discouraging would-be investors from the steamship company.

But, in the cut-throat world of business, being proved right counts for nothing if others are quicker to take up on your innovations than you are.

North Atlantic shipping companies in both London and Liverpool had watched the coming together of the *Great Western* with immense interest, and as it entered its final stages of completion, began to convert existing ships in order that they could compete with her.

The British & American Steam Navigation Company's new vessel, the *British Queen*, would not pip the *Great Western* to the post as regards making a maiden voyage, and so the firm hired another ship, the

703-ton *Sirius*, with which it intended to make the first scheduled steamship crossing to the United States. The *Sirius* set out with 22 passengers in March 1838, while the engines on the *Great Western* were still being tested.

At last, on 31 March, the *Great Western* set off for Bristol with Isambard on board to collect the passengers for her maiden voyage. However, around noon, with the ship moving down the Thames, flames and smoke began pouring from the engine room. The boiler lagging had become too hot and caught fire.

The ship's captain, Lieut Hosken, grounded the *Great Western* on soft mud while the fire was extinguished, but Isambard, descending a ladder to the boiler room, stepped on a burned rung and fell 20ft, badly injuring himself.

The *Great Western* arrived in Bristol on 2 April, only to find that many of the passengers had cancelled their

bookings because of rumours, which had spread about the ship's 'failings'.

With just seven passengers on board, the *Great Western* set out in pursuit of the *Sirius* on 7 April. It arrived in New York at noon on 23 April, having made the crossing in just 17 days – only to see the *Sirius*, which had run aground there the previous night, after exhausting almost all of its coal supply – already moored there.

The Americans were enthralled by the race between the two ships, and so many people wanted to board the *Great Western* that the captain was forced to issue tickets in order to control numbers. On the return journey, the *Great Western* reached Britain in just 14 days, as compared to the 18 taken by her rival, and proved that unlike its competitor, it could cross the Atlantic with passengers and cargo and still have coal to spare.

The *Great Western* proved to be another world-beater for Isambard, and was an immediate commercial success, making 67 crossings in eight years and silencing her critics for good.

However, she could not fit through the lock gates leading into the Floating Harbour, and accrued high

Above: The *SS Great Britain* is now the jewel in the crown of the waterfront where it was built, and is a focal point for the Brunel 200 celebrations in 2006.
BRISTOL TOURISM

mooring charges by having to be moored in King's Road in the Bristol Channel.

When it left Bristol for New York on 11 February 1843, it would be the last departure of a transatlantic liner from the port for 28 years. In turn, Bristol's importance as a port for Atlantic trade went into decline, and all because the harbour authorities refused to widen the lock gates for new, bigger ships to pass.

Taken out of service at Liverpool in 1846, the *Great Western* was sold to the Royal Mail Steam Packet Company and used on voyages to the Gulf of Mexico for 10 years, after which she ended her days as a troop ship during the Crimean War, before being scrapped in 1857.

Never one to take a well-deserved rest, in September 1838, Isambard and his committee began planning their second ship.

Initial thoughts by Isambard, Guppy and Claxton turned to a bigger 254ft-long oak ship with even bigger paddle wheels, but they were stopped in their tracks when an iron-hulled paddle steamer, the *Rainbow*, docked in Bristol. Claxton and Paterson sailed in the ship to Antwerp to record her performance.

The first iron-hulled vessel had appeared in 1787, a 70ft-long canal barge, built by John 'Iron Mad' Wilkinson, a partner in the successful project to build the world's first iron bridge over the Severn Gorge, and who, on his death in 1808, was buried in his native Cumberland in an iron coffin.

Medium-sized ocean-going iron-hulled ships were being produced in Britain in the 1820s, and had the advantage of being 30 per cent lighter than their wooden counterparts. The first iron steamship, the *Aaron Derby*, was built in 1821, but was on nowhere near the scale proposed by Isambard for the company's second ship.

The Brunel committee sat down to work, and between September 1838 and June the following year, six different designs were produced. Eventually chosen was Isambard's 'box-girder' type hull with a two-skinned cellular construction, having six watertight compartments and two longitudinal bulkheads, plus a strong iron deck.

The keel for the new vessel, nicknamed the 'Mammoth' was laid on 19 July 1839, again in Patterson's yard.

Isambard was captivated by the sight of the world's first propeller-driven ship, Francis Pettit Smith's *Archimedes*, when it arrived in the Floating Harbour in May 1840, and Guppy took a trip to Liverpool aboard her.

His report impressed the steamship company to the extent that they ordered all work on the paddle steamers for their second vessel to stop, and booked the *Archimedes* for six months of tests.

Isambard saw that a fully immersed propeller would be far more efficient than paddle wheels, and in December 1840 insisted that the new ship should be driven exclusively by one.

The decision delivered a fatal blow to ambitious young engineer, Francis Humphrys, who had been chosen by the directors above Maudslay (and against Isambard's advice) to build what would have been the world's biggest marine engine for the ship as originally planned. Told to redesign the paddle engines, which were already at an advanced stage, he resigned and died of a 'brain fever' a few days after his work was halted.

Without an engine for the new ship, the project was delayed for two years while Brunel and Smith carried out more research into propellers. During this time, they designed an 800-ton experimental sloop, the *Rattler*, for the Navy. During a tug-of-war contest in April 1845, when attached to the *Alecto*, a paddle-driven vessel of similar size, the *Rattler* towed it backwards at a speed of more than two knots. Isambard had backed the winning horse yet again.

With Humphrys gone, Isambard designed the 1600-horsepower engines himself, based on the triangle type patented by his father. The company had leased land next to the Floating Harbour and developed the site into the world's first integrated steamship works, building the engines inside.

The cost of the project soared, ending up at £125,555 – double that of the *Great Western*, but, buoyed by the success of his GWR, Isambard's project managed to attract sufficient investors.

The ship was launched on 19 July 1843, exactly six years after that of the *Great Western*.

Prince Albert, arrived from London via the GWR on a special train driven by Daniel Gooch to take his place as guest of honour, after being greeted by the Lord Mayor at Temple Meads station.

Marc and Sophia Brunel watched proudly as the dry dock was flooded to allow their son's giant creation to float.

Mrs Miles was again brought forward to name the ship, but the bottle of champagne missed its target. Prince Albert stepped forward to complete the job and smash a second bottle on the bow, naming the ship the *SS Great Britain* – a flagship for a country in a world it was beginning to dominate through its empire.

After the ceremony, the *SS Great Britain* was moved back into the dry dock for fitting out. She was ready in March 1844, but then it was discovered that she was too big to pass through the locks, which linked the Floating Harbour to the Avon estuary.

Isambard was the dock company's consulting engineer, and persuaded its directors to allow modifications to be made to allow the *SS Great Britain* to pass the Junction Lock into Cumberland Basin, which it did on 26 October 1844, after a delicate and daunting day-long operation.

Trials were undertaken in the Bristol Channel on 12 December and 10 and 20 January before the *SS Great Britain* made a 40-hour voyage to London on 23 January, averaging 12½ knots, despite bad weather.

She was moored on the Thames for five months; Queen Victoria and Prince Albert were given a guided tour of the ship on 22 April 1845. With a displacement of 3675 tons, compared to 2300 for the *Great Western*, the *SS Great Britain* was the biggest ship in the world.

auctioned off all of her fixtures and fittings before finally selling her to Liverpool shipping firm Bright, Gibbs & Co for a knockdown £18,000.

The Great Western Steamship Company was wound up in February 1852 and the lease on its dockyard sold to Patterson.

New engines were installed for the *Great Western's* comeback voyage in May 1852, after which the ship spent 24 successful years working the route to Australia. In 1876 she was bought by Antony Gibbs, Sons & Co for use as a transatlantic cargo sailing ship.

After difficulties rounding Cape Horn in April 1886, during which two masts were lost and severe leaks sprung, shelter was sought at Port Stanley in the Falkland Islands.

Estimates for repairs proved too costly, and the ship was sold to the Falkland Islands Company as a store ship for coal and wood.

In 1937, the SS *Great Britain* was towed out of the harbour and beached at Sparrow Cove, with holes knocked in her stern to ensure that she would never float again.

Thankfully, that was not the end of the story.

The pioneers of transport preservation have made great advances in the post-war decades, not only in the fields of railway and canal heritage and the saving of historic aircraft, but also in shipping.

Interest in saving the SS *Great Britain* started in the USA and England during the 1950s, and in 1968, a naval architect visited the Falklands to see if it was possible to refloat her.

It was indeed possible, with the aid of a pontoon submerged beneath her hull. With the pontoon pumped out, the ship lifted on top of it.

The SS *Great Britain* was able to make one last voyage atop the pontoon, making the 7000 miles home, towed behind the salvage tug *Varius II*.

The journey began on 24 April 1970, via Montevideo, and took until 22 June, when they arrived off the Welsh coast, where Bristol tugs were waiting to take the pontoon into the docks at Avonmouth.

The SS *Great Britain* received a hero's welcome in the port, and soon after, was lifted off the pontoon in the graving dock.

Finally, on 5 July, thousands of spectators again lined the banks of the Avon estuary as the ship, now afloat in its own right, was towed upstream to Bristol's docks. She waited a fortnight for a spring tide high enough to allow her to be eased into the Great Western dry dock off the Floating Harbour.

The date was 19 July, 127 years to the day that she was launched in 1843.

The meticulous restoration of the SS *Great Britain*, which is now recognised as having begun a revolution in international shipping, took 35 years to complete, and it is now a major attraction for tourists who come to see her in dry dock on one of the world's greatest waterfronts. The construction of a 'glass sea' at the waterline of the restored ship acts as a giant airtight chamber protecting its lower hull. Beneath the glass plate, moisture is removed from the air using special dehumidification equipment, preventing further corrosion of the hull. What was once the world's biggest ship is now encased in one of the world's biggest display cases.

The 'glass sea' is covered with a thin layer of water, so the ship appears to be floating. However, visitors can descend beneath the glass to see the ship's hull and its key component, the propeller.

It will now stay moored in the dry dock, as a lasting monument to a man who shrank the world with his vision of transatlantic travel.

Its first Atlantic crossing was made from Liverpool on 26 July, carrying only 45 passengers and arriving in New York just 15 days later at an average speed of more than nine knots. During her second trip to the USA, the SS *Great Britain* sustained damage to the propeller and returned to Liverpool under sail power only, but still in only 20 days.

A four-bladed propeller replaced Isambard's experimental six-bladed version, and a third voyage was made to New York on 29 May 1846. On the homeward journey, the SS *Great Britain* made the crossing in just 13 days, at an average speed of 13 knots.

The ship's fifth trip, however, was an unmitigated disaster. With 180 passengers on board, it ran aground in Dundrum Bay in Ireland, on 22 September, with Captain Hosken, claiming his instruments had been affected by the iron hull and leading him to believe that he was off the coast of the Isle of Man.

There were no fatalities, and while the ship had been holed in two places, its strength prevented it from breaking up.

Claxton built a succession of two breakwaters around the beached ship to protect her, but to no avail, and with the finances of the steamship company also sailing close to the wind, Isambard finally went out to Ireland, to order a protective barrier of 5000 faggots to be piled against the side of the ship, which faced the sea.

After many efforts, the SS *Great Britain* was finally towed off the beach, by HMS *Birkenhead* on 27 August 1847.

However, its owners could not afford the £22,000 repairs on top of the £12,670 towing charge, and

      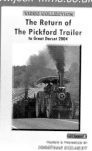

HOW THE WEST WAS FINALLY WON

The bridge at Saltash and beyond

In 814AD, the Saxons under Egbert conquered Cornwall, the last Celtic kingdom in the south-west, although he left the native rules in place. A century later, King Alfred's grandson, Athelstan, made an all-out effort to bring Cornwall under English rule, but it would not be so easily tamed.

The River Tamar remained, for the most part, not only a great physical divide but a psychological and cultural one too. Cornishmen often thought of their homeland as a separate country, referring to Devon as 'England'.

Nine hundred years later, the Tamar remained the last frontier for the great transport pioneers to conquer in order to bring the railway into the Duchy, where it would serve the mineral-rich mining areas and convey their products to markets far and wide.

The word Tamar is far older than English or Cornish. It has its roots in the ancient Sanskrit word for dark, which also presents itself in other British river names such as Tame, Teme, Thame, and Thames.

Just as Isambard had conquered the Thames with bridges everyone who knew better said would never stand up, so he was to accomplish what nobody else had ever believed possible – master the Tamar at its widest point.

Before the mid-19th century, the lowest crossing of the river was at New Bridge at Gunnislake, a local mining town. It was by then not so new, having been built in 1520 to carry the road from Callington to Tavistock.

If you wanted to cross below this point, such as from Plymouth to Torpoint or Saltash, boat was the only way. Until Isambard Brunel appeared, with his determination to turn one of his greatest dreams into reality – to run a railway from Paddington to Penzance.

The Cornwall Railway was promoted in late 1844, just after Brunel had completed the Bristol & Exeter Railway. Captain William Moorsom, who had been involved with the Bristol & Gloucester Railway eight years previously, was asked by local businessmen in 1843 to survey a line and draw up plans for a 66-mile line from the South Devon Railway at Plymouth to the naval port of Falmouth.

He talked of a 'floating bridge' or train ferry to cross the Hamoaze, the name given to the estuary of the tidal Tamar opposite Devonport, and had at first considered to work the Cornish line by atmospheric propulsion.

After the first scheme was thrown out by the House of Lords, Isambard replaced Moorsom and was appointed engineer for the project, and carried out a new survey, this time calling for a high-level bridge across the Tamar.

This vastly improved plan was passed by Parliament on 3 August 1846, and as expected, Isambard opted again for broad gauge.

An alternative 1845 proposal for a Central Cornwall Railway, taking the time-honoured coach road through the middle of the county, and backed by the GWR's great rival-to-be, the London & South Western Railway, failed to win approval.

However, while drawing up that scheme, the LSWR had bought out Cornwall's first public railway, the Bodmin & Wadebridge, in the vain hope of using it as part of the route. The action left the LSWR with a 'white elephant' to which it would not connect for 40 years, but it dashed Cornwall Railway's hopes of a broad-gauge branch to the port of Padstow.

Work on the Cornwall Railway began at Truro in 1847, but little work was done for several years because money kept running out. This was the time when the first great wave of Railway Mania was beginning to falter and backers for schemes were becoming scarce.

Meanwhile, further west in the Duchy, the standard-gauge Hayle Railway opened in 1837, running from Hayle Foundry to Pool and Portreath, and extending to Redruth the following year. Its primary aim was to connect the Redruth-Camborne mining areas to the coast, and steam locomotives were used from the start over most of its system.

On 3 August 1846, the West Cornwall Railway received authorisation and took over the Hayle Railway, intending eventually, to convert it to broad gauge, extend it to Penzance in one direction and Truro in the other, thereby meeting up with the future Cornwall Railway. Isambard was brought in as engineer on the West Cornwall too, and became chairman of its board from 1847-8.

Under Isambard's jurisdiction, the West Cornwall

The River Tamar remained, for the most part, not only a great physical divide but a psychological and cultural one too.

was completed between Penzance and a temporary Truro terminus in 1851, opening on 11 March 1852.

While mineral traffic on the line was of paramount importance, the West Cornwall opened up the prospect of easier travel to London for those living at the far end of the county for the first time. You could travel from Penzance or Truro to Hayle, take the paddle steamer packet service on to Bristol and travel onwards by the GWR.

Isambard's Cornwall Railway route involved no fewer than 34 viaducts over the 53 miles between Plymouth and Truro, each built in timber, just like several that had been on the later sections of the South Devon Railway, including the 670ft-long Ivybridge Viaduct, and also the 1760ft Landore Viaduct in South Wales.

Nine more were to follow on the West Cornwall, as a total of eight river estuaries and 30 valleys were crossed.

His distinctive trestle structures – known as fan viaducts because of the shape of the supports –

involved timber constructions of masonry pillars, and were a cost-effective way of crossing the steep Cornish terrain.

These were far longer and more complex than his first timber bridge, a five-span affair, which carried a public road across Sonning cutting.

Although they were all were replaced from the late 19th century onwards with more expensive and longer-lasting stone alternatives, the old columns can still be seen standing alongside the new crossings at places like Moorswater.

Mindful of criticism that wood, mainly Baltic pine, could rot away, the viaducts were designed by Brunel in such a way that any offending timbers could be unbolted and replaced without having to close the line. Many of them lasted for 60 years, and it was only after the price of timber became too high after the outbreak of WWI that there was a mass movement to replace them with masonry.

The last to survive in Cornwall was College Wood Viaduct on the Falmouth branch, which stayed in situ until 1934.

In a bid to revive the stalled project, following years in the financial doldrums, Isambard announced in 1851 that he had found contractors to build the Cornwall Railway for £800,000, albeit single rather than double track, but the offer was not taken up. Hopes rose again when contracts for the key Plymouth-Saltash section were placed the following year.

The GWR, Bristol & Exeter and South Devon Railway took on a partial lease of the project from 1855, and continued to bail it out as construction proceeded in piecemeal fashion.

It was left to Isambard to tackle the biggest hurdle of them all – the Tamar, which at Saltash is 1100ft wide and 70ft deep.

At first he suggested building a timber bridge with one main span of 255ft and six further spans of 105ft each, but the Navy insisted that any crossing must allow headroom of 100ft to clear the masts of tall ships.

He then suggested a single-span bridge to clear the estuary in one fell swoop, but the estimated £500,000 cost was way beyond the reaches of the Cornwall Railway.

Isambard then came up with a truly stunning and radical design, which more than made up for his disastrous fling with atmospheric propulsion, a mode by now long deleted from the Cornwall Railway scheme.

His Tamar crossing featured two arched tubular girders, fastened to four cast-iron columns in the middle of the river, supporting by suspension a pair of 450ft spans, which would carry a single-track railway from one side of the river to another – a double-track version had been slimmed down, again to save money.

After test borings beneath the mud of the riverbed, a huge wrought-iron cylinder was sunk in the middle of the estuary, after a highly complex and elaborate operation.

Inside, workmen toiled away in hellish conditions at the bed of the river, digging down to the rock strata so that a solid granite column could be fixed in it. The column supports the cast-iron pillars supporting the great tubular arches.

Isambard drew much from his design for the Usk Bridge at Chepstow, and his use of tubular steel harked back to the far humbler swing bridge at Bristol's Floating Harbour.

The tubular girders were assembled on the east bank and weighed 1060 tons when finished. They were

Above: All alone – before the coming of the modern suspension bridge, Brunel's rail crossing of the Tamar as seen in the early 20th century. ROBIN JONES COLLECTION

Left: This third section of a Cornwall Railway broad-gauge coach from the mid-19th century ended up being used as a track ganger's hut in Grampound Road, from where it was retrieved by National Railway Museum staff in 1977 and restored for display at its headquarters in York. ROBIN JONES

floated across the river into position on pontoons, after a special dock was cut in the Devon bank, and jacked up with hydraulic presses to the required height; this truly spectacular operation began on 1 September 1857.

Attached to each tube were the suspension chains, linked to each other by 11 uprights. Diagonal bracing was added to provide extra rigidity.

Isambard had gained vast experience in lifting suspension bridges when he assisted Robert Stephenson in the construction of the Conway and Britannia bridges in North Wales.

The great bridge, which has an overall length of 730 yards, took seven years to build and cost £225,000. Despite the colossal expense by the day's standards, the directors of the Cornwall Railway heaped praise on him, knowing that it would outlive their lifetimes and

many more, acknowledging that it was nonetheless a truly economic solution.

After his death, the inscription, I K BRUNEL ENGINEER 1859, was ordered to be displayed above the entry arches in perpetuity. Everyone who travelled to Cornwall and passed through the unique structure would immediately be told the name of its designer.

By the time the bridge was finished, the remainder of the Plymouth-Truro line had been completed, all ready for the first trains.

The structure was named the Royal Albert Bridge, as it was the Prince Consort who opened it officially on 2 May 1859.

Both banks of the river were packed with onlookers, while others crowded on hills and rooftops overlooking the river, desperate for a glimpse of the proceedings. A

Above: An *Illustrated London News* view of the newly opened Royal Saltash Bridge.
BRUNEL 200

Right: A view of St Ives station with a fine array of broad-gauge wagons on show.
BROAD GAUGE SOCIETY

Old Wood Viaduct,
St. Georges Road.   Truro.

flotilla of steamers and small boats plied their way up the Hamoaze for a grandstand view. The last county in Britain without a link to the national rail network was now connected.

VIPs from Cornwall, including the mayors of Truro and Penzance, arrived by train and were presented to the prince. The following day, a grand civic banquet was held in the Town Hall at Truro to serve guests who had arrived on a special train, which left Plymouth at 10.30am and arrived shortly before 1pm.

It was said that everyone living in the towns and villages along the route had turned out to cheer and wave the train on as it passed.

On 4 May, the Cornwall Railway was opened to the public. At last the county, which had produced Richard Trevithick, inventor of the first railway locomotive, was connected to the national network, and thereby to London. The world had suddenly grown much smaller, and the Tamar was, for the first time in history, no more a barrier.

One important person was sadly absent from the opening celebrations. Isambard Brunel.

In deteriorating health, he was too ill to attend, but did manage to ride across the bridge a few days later, lying couch mounted, on a truck pulled by a Gooch engine.

The final part of the original Cornwall Railway route, from Truro to Falmouth, had to wait another four years

Top: A colour postcard of Brunel's viaduct in Truro, highlighting the typical fan-like construction of the supports. Although replaced in 1902, five of the piers survive in Victoria Gardens. These 'cheap' yet sturdy viaducts enabled the Plymouth to Penzance lines to be built. BROAD GAUGE SOCIETY

Above left: Lelant on the St Ives branch, the last passenger-carrying line to be built to Brunel's broad gauge. BROAD GAUGE SOCIETY

before it was opened. Work had begun in 1850, but stopped when the contractor failed. Renewed calls for its completion were made loudly in 1861 when new docks at Falmouth were completed, and it finally opened on 24 August 1863.

By then, however, Falmouth had declined in importance in transport terms, with the Royal Mail Packet Service fleet having been transferred from here to Southampton, after more than 150 years. The result was that the line to Truro would remain a branch line, not the intended main line, which now ran on to Penzance.

In 1864, the Cornwall Railway exercised its right to demand that the West Cornwall, which was still standard gauge, laid a broad-gauge rail to accommodate through trains. It could not afford it, and so it was leased to the consortium of the GWR, Bristol & Exeter and South Devon Railway, which immediately laid the third rail.

At last, on 1 March 1867, a through service between Paddington and Penzance was begun, with locomotives supplied by the South Devon Railway. At last, the great dream of those who had launched the GWR more than a third of a century before had been realised, and the future tourist trade of the West Country was assured.

Furthermore two subsequent offshoots of the West Cornwall deserve special mention.

A branch nearly five miles long from St Erth on the mainline, to St Ives was authorised in 1876 and opened on 1 June 1877. It was the last new Brunel broad-gauge line to be built, and became the property of the GWR the following year.

The short standard-gauge Hayle Wharf branch had a third rail added when it was extended along the quaysides, and opened for goods traffic only on 3 October 1877.

Cornwall is famous for its sunsets, and here was the twilight of Isambard's 7ft 0¼in gauge empire, which had

stretched from London, north to Wolverhampton and westwards to Milford Haven and now Penzance.

The Royal Albert Bridge has been strengthened several times since it was built, and the station at Saltash at the western end still retains its original 1859 building.

In the Macmillan years when we 'never had it so good,' the car became king as more and more people could afford to buy one, and as a result many West Country branch lines began to close, even before Dr Richard Beeching wielded his axe in 1963.

The following year, a second Tamar crossing was opened alongside Brunel's, a modern suspension bridge taking the A38 from Plymouth to Saltash, replacing the car ferry that ran below.

Above: A Class 37 diesel on the Looe branch in the 1980s at Moorswater. Note the surviving stumps of Brunel's Cornwall Railway wooden trestle viaduct rear in front of the later replacement. BRIAN SHARPE

Right: The wooden viaduct on the South Devon Railway main line at Ivybridge was typical of the type which made the building of Brunel's Cornwall Railway economically possible. BROAD GAUGE SOCIETY

THE GREAT EASTERN

The final epitaph

Isambard Brunel wasn't a man to be discouraged. Barely had the Great Western Steamship Company been wound up in 1852, after selling off the SS *Great Britain* in the wake of its Dundrum Bay disaster, but he was back at work drawing up plans for a far bigger steamship.

William Hawes, chairman of the Australian Royal Mail Company, appointed Isambard as consultant engineer to the newly formed shipping line, giving him a brief to build a vessel which would need to refuel only once en route, at Cape Town.

In turn, Isambard called on the services of an old friend, highly acclaimed naval architect, John Scott Russell, a key figure in the building of the Crystal Palace and secretary of the Royal Society of Arts, to produce the design for the steamship to his specifications.

Isambard came up with the idea for a ship with a displacement of between 5000 and 6000 tons, which the company said was too big. Instead, they opted for two smaller ships, also built to Brunel specification and Scott-Russell design, the Adelaide and the Victoria. The pair, built at Scott-Russell's Millwall shipyard, were ordered at the time of the Australian gold rush, when it seemed that a regular service would more than pay its way.

Privately, Isambard began working on a plan for a far bigger ship, which would be capable of running a regular service to either India or Australia.

His plan involved a ship 600ft long; nearly double the length of the SS *Great Britain*.

Russell and Isambard's old steamship colleague Christopher Claxton helped him develop the design, which would have a displacement of up to 21,000 tons, an engine of at least 850 horsepower, a bunker to store up to 10,000 tons of coal and capable of averaging 15 knots.

Isambard also came up with the notion of using a combination of a propeller and paddle wheels.

Such a design would be pushing the technology of the day to its limits, but any distant warnings from the ghost of the atmospheric railway went unheeded.

The Eastern Steam Navigation Company, which had been looking at running services to India, China and Australia, was receptive to Isambard's design, which was presented to them by Scott Russell. The proposal split the company's board, with some directors quitting over it, while others were lured by the prospect of massive profits to be made from a gargantuan cargo carrier.

The company went for it, and Isambard was appointed engineer. As he tried to interest investors in subscribing to the project, the company was insisting that work could only start when £800,000, or 40,000 shares had been invested.

...The ship utilised a new design of hull, one that featured girders running between an inner and outer skin...

Contracts for the ship were finally signed on 22 December 1853, with Scott Russell successfully tendering to build the ship for £377,200.

Russell's shipyard was deemed too small for the monster ship to be built inside it, and, as the company could not afford to build a berth for the project, space was leased in David Napier & Company's yard next door.

Building work began in the spring of 1854. The ship utilised a new design of hull, one that featured girders running between an inner and outer skin. It was to be 680ft long, with an 83ft beam.

In February 1856, Scott Russell went broke, and creditors took over his business, with only half the hull built.

The Eastern Steam Navigation Company then took over both the ship and the Napier yard and resumed work. Scott Russell stayed on as one of Isambard's assistants and greatly furthered progress on the project. However, Isambard was displeased that Scott Russell had made decisions on his own, while he'd been in charge, during the former's absence through illness.

A major disagreement between them led to Scott Russell taking a holiday, never to return to the Eastern Steam Navigation Company, and leaving Isambard in sole charge of the 1200-strong workforce.

There had been much debate between Isambard and Scott Russell on how the ship should be launched. Scott Russell had wanted to slide it down greased-timber

Above: Brunel's mighty ship was launched in 1859, and grossing 18,915 tons, it held the record for the largest ship ever constructed for 43 years. WESSEX WATER HISTORICAL ARCHIVE

Opposite: This photograph of Isambard Kingdom Brunel, complete with cigar, was taken at Napier's yard, in the Isle of Dogs, in November 1857. He is standing alongside the great chains used for launching the *Great Eastern*. SS GREAT BRITAIN TRUST

Left: *SS Great Eastern* on its maiden voyage as painted by Samual Walters. SS GREAT BRITAIN TRUST

launching ways, in its wooden cradle – the time-honoured way. Isambard was concerned that there would be insufficient control, and in autumn 1856 had iron plates fixed to the underside of the cradles, with iron rails laid on the launching ways.

By November 1857, the hull was ready and Isambard wanted to test the launching system. Huge chains were fastened to the launching cradles and linked to massive steam winches on Thames barges. The idea was that once the ship began to slide, its movement would be restrained by the weight of the huge chains wound on to drums.

The hull would be lowered to the low-water mark, and would float when the tide came in.

As expected, a massive crowd turned out to witness the launch, for which the cash-strapped company had sold tickets. The event began with the official naming, with Miss Hope, daughter of the company chairman, breaking a bottle over the bow.

She named the vessel, but disaster struck when the crew operating the winch drum restraining the hull's stern, diverted their attention momentarily, and its handle spun out of control. A labourer was thrown into the air as the hull lurched forward 4ft. He died of his injuries a few days later, and four others were also injured.

A second attempt to launch the behemoth failed the same day, and what was worse; the whole debacle had taken place in full view of the crowd.

Isambard brought more hydraulic presses and rams to the yard and eventually, on 31 January 1858, the ship was floated and then moored off Deptford.

By this time, costs had escalated to £600,000, well above Scott Russell's low tender – and a further £100,000 was needed to install the engines. The launch had also cost £120,000.

Everyone had lost money in the venture, and

Isambard had been so determined to finish building the ship that he allowed his health to suffer.

In may 1858, Isambard and his wife Mary took a holiday in Switzerland in a bid to recuperate, but he was not well enough to return for Queen Victoria's visit to the ship the following month.

By the time he came home in the autumn, the Eastern Steam Navigation Company was looking for a way out.

A new firm, the Great Ship Company, was formed, and in buying the hull for £165,000, it allowed the ESN to be wound up.

Despite his failing health – a kidney ailment - Isambard eagerly accepted the position of engineer to the new firm.

Coincidentally, while he spent that winter convalescing in the Mediterranean, travelling on to Egypt and Cairo, he met up with none other than Robert Stephenson. Meanwhile, the new company began fitting out the hull – and accepted a tender to do so from Scott Russell, who by this time had recovered his business.

The paddle engines were tried out in July 1859, and Isambard, his health deteriorating rapidly – his illness having been only too apparent at the opening of the Royal Albert Bridge at Saltash at the beginning of May – attended whenever he could.

He was unable to turn up for a celebratory banquet on board, organised by Scott Russell on 5 August, but he remained determined that nothing would stop him from going on the maiden voyage.

Isambard visited the ship on 2 September, but after two hours, he collapsed and had to be taken home. He had suffered a heart attack.

The maiden voyage was finally set for 7 September, and the *Great Eastern*, as it was by then known, moved from her moorings and headed off down the Thames

bound for Weymouth and Holyhead.

Isambard was confined to bed in his Duke Street house, but nonetheless insisted on receiving news of his ship, which brought out the crowds as it passed every south-coast town.

He even wrote to the Great Western Railway

directors asking them to give all the workers at Swindon the day off, along with special passes so they could ride to Weymouth, in Dorset, by train and see his ship when it arrived.

It was the last letter he ever wrote.

Around 6pm on the evening of 8 September, when the ship was off Dungeness, an almighty explosion caused the ship's forward funnel to fly 30ft into the air, along with a huge cloud of smoke and steam.

Five stokers were killed and others seriously injured. A stopcock on a water pre-heater on the funnel had been left shut, allowing pressure to build up and cause the explosion.

The *Great Eastern* was not badly damaged, and continued her journey the following morning, arriving in Weymouth, as scheduled, on 10 September.

Dismayed, Isambard heard about the tragedy that same day.

On 15 September, he called his family together for the last time, and died a few hours later, aged only 53.

His funeral, attended by a large contingent of GWR workers, along with his many friends and admirers, took place at London's Kensal Green cemetery, five days later.

The greatest of engineers was laid to rest in the same tomb as his mother and father.

He never saw the fruits of the last of his labours, which many believed had killed him.

The *Great Eastern* was technologically everything Isambard had hoped she would be, and although she never ran on the routes to the Far East as the company that began the project had planned, she did steer a more valuable course, setting guidelines and standards for the future of shipbuilding.

It was not, however, a financial success. The *Great Eastern* sustained extensive damage in a storm off the south of Ireland on September 1861, while it had 400

Above: The *Great Eastern* being launched. SS GREAT BRITAIN TRUST

Left: The funnel/ strainer, the only remnant of Brunel's *Great Eastern*, was removed from the Sutton Poyntz pumping station reservoir in 2003 and is seen on its way to the SS Great Britain Museum in Bristol. The holes drilled in the funnel in 1860 to convert it into a strainer, can be clearly seen. WESSEX WATER HISTORICAL ARCHIVE

passengers on board. The great storm damaged both the screw and the rudder, while the raging seas destroyed the paddle floats, leaving the *Great Eastern* helpless for three days.

Temporary repairs made by the crew helped her to return to Queenstown, in Ireland, where it was obvious that Isambard's design had kept her afloat in a storm that would have sunk any other vessel.

The Great Ship Company went into liquidation five years after the launch, and on 14 January 1864, the *Great Eastern* was offered for auction, but failed to sell.

In April that year she was chartered to the Telegraph Construction Company to lay the first transatlantic telegraph cable between Europe and North America, a job which was completed on 1 September 1866.

The entrepreneur who led the venture - and was knighted for dooing so - was none other than Isambard's locomotive superintendent Daniel Gooch!

Isambard would have been proud.

In 1867, his ship briefly went back to carrying passengers and when it departed from Liverpool for New York on 26 March, it was carrying the science-fiction writer Jules Verne and his brother Paul.

The *Great Eastern*, however, was far more commercially successfully as a cable layer, and in 1869, was chartered to lay the French transatlantic cable. In February 1870, she laid a cable between Bombay and Aden, in Yemen, in a fortnight.

In 1886, the *Great Eastern* was sold at auction for use as a floating fair and an advertising hoarding.

The following year, she was bought at an auction in Greenock, near Inverness, by ship breakers who moved her to Liverpool for dismantling, a process that began in May 1889 and lasted 18 months.

The only remaining piece of the ship's structure is a section of funnel, which was adapted for use as a strainer at the Sutton Poyntz pumping station reservoir, near Weymouth, after the stricken *Great Eastern* had docked at the port for repairs in 1859.

In 2003, it was removed from the reservoir and donated by Wessex Water to the *SS Great Britain* Museum in Bristol, where it remains today.

**Above The stricken *Great Eastern* in Weymouth Bay in 1859.
This rare stereo-card photograph shows the *Great Eastern*, after the explosion on 9 September 1859, moored and awaiting repairs – minus the forward (No 1) funnel.**
WESSEX WATER HISTORICAL ARCHIVE

Top: A contemporary illustration of the explosion which rocked the *Great Eastern* at Dungeness, and the fallen funnel afterwards. SS GREAT BRITAIN TRUST

Middle: The funnel of the *Great Eastern* lies on its deck following the explosion.
SS GREAT BRITAIN TRUST

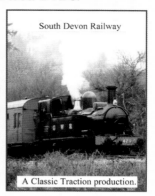

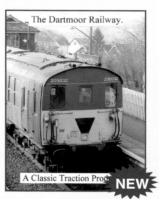

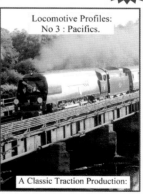

1892
Victory of the narrow minded

Its inventor and champion gone, it seemed that there would be little standing between Isambard's broad gauge and oblivion. However, it lingered on for a third of a century after his death, and nearly half a century after the Gauge Commission came down in favour of standard gauge, despite the facts in its favour.

It was the breaks of gauge that caused most concern, with more than 30 recorded in South Wales alone. As the smaller standard-gauge railway companies began to merge into large ones, more mixed-gauge lines were laid over part of the Great Western system. Mixed-gauge operation finally reached the heart of the broad-gauge system, Paddington, in August 1861.

When he became chairman, Daniel Gooch, who had been the most passionate supporter of Brunel's broad gauge three decades before, no longer swam against an unstoppable tide, and instead moved towards large-scale conversion of GWR routes to standard gauge.

The first such gauge conversions took place in 1866, when broad gauge extended to 1427 miles, including 387 miles of mixed gauge. First to go were the lines north of Oxford by 1869 followed by the conversion of the South Wales main line in 1872. By 1873 around 200 route-miles in Berkshire, Wiltshire, Hampshire and Somerset had been changed over. The 'dinosaur', however, still insisted on giving birth, even on the brink of extinction, the aforementioned St Ives branch opening as broad gauge in 1877.

As more broad-gauge lines were converted, there became less investment in 7ft 0¼in gauge locomotives and stock.

The Bristol & Exeter opened its Cheddar Valley line from Yatton to Wells in 1869; when it was converted to standard gauge in November 1875, it became not only one of the shortest-lived broad-gauge lines of all, but the only part of the BER to be converted prior to absorption by the GWR two months later.

The last broad-gauge engine was outshopped from Swindon, Rover class 4-2-2 No 24 *Tornado*, in July 1888. By way of contrast, it had built its first standard-gauge engines in 1855, a year after absorbing its first 4ft 8½in lines, the Shrewsbury & Chester, and Shrewsbury & Birmingham railways.

Gooch died in 1889, and afterwards the final conversion was planned – that of the Paddington-Penzance main line in its 177-mile entirety.

The operation was planned to the exact detail, with the general manager at Paddington issuing 80 pages of instructions on how it should be done.

Track work was prepared for removal and new rails and sleepers brought in ready, while standard-gauge locomotives and coaches were moved to strategic points

along the great route on broad-gauge wagons.

D-Day was named as Saturday 21 May 1892, when more than 4200 tracklayers gathered along the line, after the last broad-gauge engines had steamed back to Swindon to be herded into 15 miles of temporary sidings on a three-acre site, bought especially to store them pending scrapping. A total of 196 engines, 347 coaches and 3544 wagons survived to the end.

The last broad-gauge train from Paddington was the 5pm to Plymouth on the Friday, hauled by Rover class locomotives *Bulkeley* to Bristol and *Iron Duke* from there to Newton Abbot. *Bulkeley* also worked the final train to London, the night mail, which reached Paddington at 5.30pm on the Saturday.

The last broad-gauge train from Penzance was a 9.10pm empty stock working, hauled by two

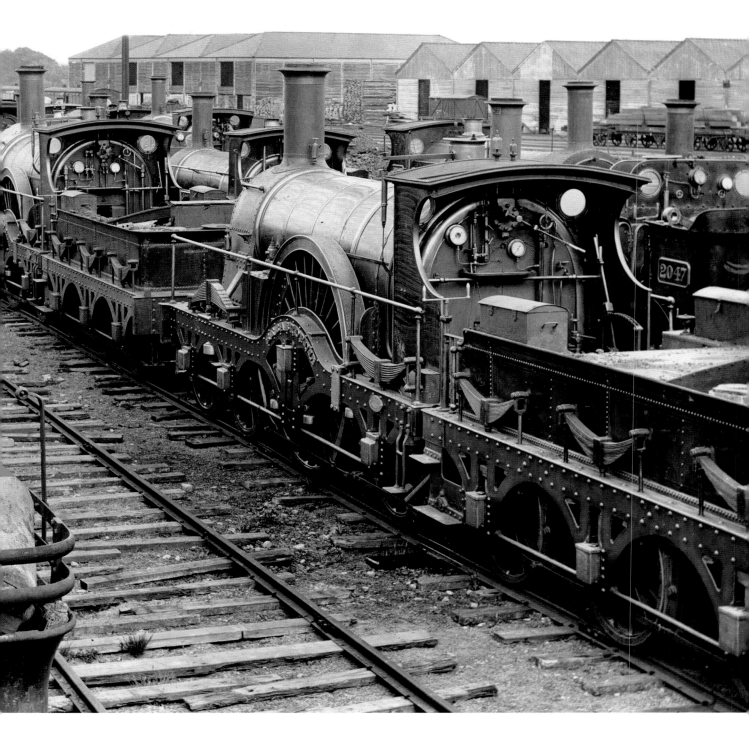

'convertible' locomotives, which would thereby escape immediate scrapping. As the last 7ft 0¼in gauge train passed through each station, the stationmaster had to confirm to the inspector aboard that there was no broad-gauge stock in his sidings.

The inspector then presented the stationmaster with a certificate, which was handed over to the line engineer as the signal to begin the conversion.

The line free of trains at last, the platelayers and gangers got down to business, the final conversion being scheduled for completion for just after 4am on the Monday.

It all went ahead as planned. Brunel would have winced at the loss of his broad gauge, but would also surely have marvelled at the mammoth operation carried out in such a short space of time with the

minimum of inconvenience to traffic.

The mail train from Penzance to Paddington, which departed Plymouth at 4.40am on the Monday, was the first to run the length of the new all standard-gauge premier route. After the curtain fell on a proud era of our railway history, it heralded a new dawn, presenting the successors to Brunel and Gooch with many exciting new challenges and successes on the Great Western Railway they had built.

The last GWR broad-gauge engines to run were South Devon Railway 4-4-0 saddle tanks *Leopard* and *Stag*. Both were used at Swindon for shunting broad-gauge stock into the cutting shop for scrapping until June 1893, when they befell the same fate. There was nowhere left for them to run.

Incidentally, broad gauge had also been employed on

Above: With nowhere left to run, rows of broad gauge locomotives await the cutter's torch at Swindon in 1892, following the end of Brunel's 7ft 0¼in gauge. The nearest on the right is Rover class 4-2-2 *Sebastopol*, who was rebuilt/renewed from an Iron Duke locomotive only four years before.
GW TRUST COLLECTION

a far smaller scale on several Victorian harbour and breakwater railways, at Holyhead, Portland and Port Erin, no doubt because of their capacity to carry bigger loads to and from ships as well as the huge stone blocks used in their construction.

These were mainly the work of engineer James Meadows Rendel (1799-1856) or inspired by his designs. He also collaborated with Isambard.

Brunel's gauge may have been the widest of any passenger-carrying system in the world, but it was not the widest to be used for freight. For instance, the Dalzell Iron & Steel Works in Motherwell was once supplied with three new Barclay 0-4-0 saddle tanks to haul ladles of molten slag on an internal 10ft11in gauge line.

The 7ft 0¼in gauge dream did not die out entirely in 1892. The engineer W Collard published plans in 1928 for a Brunel broad-gauge railway from London to Paris via a channel tunnel. What if it had been built? What if we still had broad gauge today?

Hindsight may well seem to support Brunel and Gooch's convictions. Today's larger, faster trains could have benefited from the increased flexibility of a broad-

gauge network without narrow bridges and low headroom.

On the other hand, would greater operating and maintenance costs have pushed even more customers towards cheaper road transport?

One very unsavoury convert to the Brunel vision drew up plans for a Europe-wide railway system with tracks three metres wide – 9ft 9ins – in the 1940s.

Monstrous locomotives would haul carriages, each capable of carrying hundreds of passengers, and wagons built to take ships, across a network of lines radiating from Berlin to Paris, Moscow and beyond, serving the Fatherland's newly conquered territories in a post-war world and ensuring its armies could be mobilised at a moment's notice.

Thankfully this railway never had the chance to be built, for the would-be architect of it was none other than Adolf Hitler.

Brunel broad gauge is still in commercial use in Britain today – at one location. At the Environment Agency depot in Reading, an electric crane runs when required on a 151ft-long track.

Top: Rover class locomotives Great Western, an 1880 'renewal' of the original, and Swallow, built 1871, head the 'Flying Dutchman' through Didcot in May 1892, the last month of broad gauge operation. GW TRUST COLLECTION

Above right: Temporary sidings at Swindon were crammed with broad gauge wagons following the conversion of the last part of the GWR system to standard gauge. GW TRUST COLLECTION

Kidlington Railwayana Auctions

Future Sales
At Exeter Hall, Kidlington, Nr Oxford

22nd April	7th October	20th January
2006	2006	2007

website: www.gcrauctions.com

WE NOW INVITE ENTRIES FOR THE ABOVE SALES

Following our recent highly successful sale, we now welcome entries for our future sales during 2006/2007.

Our commission rate is 10% of the sale price + VAT (total 11.75%) which includes cataloguing, photography (99% of lots colour illustrated), insured storage and advertising. We give a guaranteed payment date to vendors seven working days after each Kidlington sale. With over eighteen hundred collectors on our mailing list, we can guarantee maximum exposure for items entered in our auctions. We provide comprehensive advertising in this and other specialist magazines and on the web. In dealing with specialist railwayana auctioneers you will benefit from the highest prices, avoid the uncertainty of selling privately or on line and know that your property is being handled by experts with an intimate knowledge of this specialist field. In certain cases we can arrange collection of auction entries.

Our sales at Kidlington are held in a spacious modern venue with free parking, bar and catering and railwayana sales stands. Catalogues are available a fortnight before each Sale, free on application. These sales contain a wide cross-section of material reflecting every aspect of railway operations. We offer everything from Main Line Nameplates, Works and Number Plates to Station Signs, Lamps and Signalling Equipment. We aim to include a huge variety of rare and unusual material, not merely based on value but on interest and rarity. You will find railwayana to suit all budgets and pockets.

FOR ENTRY DETAILS PHONE FOR AN INFORMAL CHAT OR WRITE TO THE ADDRESS BELOW.

We welcome entries in, but not restricted to, the following categories:

Steam and Diesel Locomotive Nameplates
Worksplates, Builder's Plates
Smokebox Number Plates
GWR Cabside Numberplates
Shedcode Plates
Totem Station Signs
Signalbox Nameboards
(cast iron/wood/enamel)
Carriage Prints (landscapes and advertising)
Station Direction Signs
Railway Office Equipment
(inc. brass handstamps, paperweights)
Signal Line Tablets
Wagonplates
Station Lamps (wall or post mounted)
Signalbox Instruments (blocks, bells, repeaters, train describers, token / tablet instruments, others)
Signalbox Diagrams (framed/unframed)
Signal Lever Description Plates (naming locations or with unusual wordings)
Description Plates from block shelves or instruments with locations

Loco Headboards from Named Trains and Carriageboards
Signal Post Finials
Platform Seats with Company Name (inc. FR Squirrel Pattern)
Loco Whistles, Handlamps
Armbands (enamel or brass)
Badges (inc. BR totem and fishtail)
Door Plates
(cast iron / enamel inc. BR)
Posters
Silverware
Clocks and Watches
Foreign Builder's / Works Plates
Key Tokens (brass or alloy)
Seat Back Names
(cast / enamel)
Staffs (brass, steel or wooden)
Platform Ticket Machines
Bridge Number Plates
Target Station Signs
(SR/LMS/LT)
Industrial Name
/Works Plates

DIESEL AND ELECTRIC NAMEPLATES

We are always keen to include Nameplates from modern traction and offer a specialist selection of such items in each auction. There is an ever growing interest in Nameplates, Works Plates and Depot Plaques, not only from 1960s Locomotives but also more modern cast aluminium /reflective Nameplates. We are keen to include all types of modern traction plates and are particularly seeking examples from English Electric Class 40s, Peaks, D600/D800 Class Warships, Westerns, Class 47s, Class 50s and Deltics.

Kidlington Railwayana Auctions and Great Central Auctions
Operated By
Great Central Railwayana Ltd
14, School Street, Woodford Halse, Daventry, Northants, NN11 3RL
Tel: 01327 263633   (Monday to Saturday 10.30 – 7.00)
Personal callers by appointment only please.

Valuations for insurance and probate, impartial advice on selling or buying Railwayana.

ITEMS ILLUSTRATED ARE INCLUDED IN OUR APRIL AUCTION

Coat of Arms ex West Country Class Bulleid Pacific "Bude"

Highest Catalogue Circulation 2000 +

99% of Entries Illustrated in Full Colour

Commission Rate 10% + VAT (11.75% of hammer price)

Guaranteed Payment Date for Vendors 7 Working Days after Auction

Professionally Managed Website Promoting Your Entries

Coat of Arms ex West Country Class Bulleid Pacific "Seaton"

Extensive and Prominent Monthly Advertising with Listing of Entries in This and Many Other Magazines

Collection Service Available

Sales by Private Treaty Possible

Full-time Professional Staff with 20 Year's Experience with a Host of Record Prices Achieved

FIRE FLY

Brunel's steam dream reborn

AS chief mechanical engineer of the London, Midland & Scottish Railway, William Stanier designed some of the finest locomotives in the world.

Those who have seen one of the surviving examples, express passenger engine Princess Coronation 4-6-2 No 6233 *Duchess of Sutherland* in action – now a preservation icon, which hauled the Royal Train in 2002 and 2005 – will need no convincing here.

However, when it came to heritage matters, Stanier was nothing less than a vandal of the worst order.

For it was he, long before Henry Ford, who effectively declared that, 'history is bunk' – and consigned museum pieces to the scrapyard.

After the end of the broad gauge, the GWR cut up all but two of the 7ft 0¼in gauge engines.

Spared the scrapyard were pioneer *North Star*, which had been preserved after withdrawal in 1871, and celebrity Iron Duke class 4-2-2 *Lord of the Isles*, the Great Western Railway's exhibit at the Great Exhibition of 1851.

The pair appeared at various exhibitions, *Lord of the Isles* even appearing at Chicago in 1893 and Earls Court in 1897.

The GWR continued to expand, and in the early years of the 20th century, space at Swindon where the

pair were stored was at a premium.

The two survivors were offered to a succession of museums, but none could find the space to display them.

Stanier, who was then in charge of Swindon Works, decided – in the absence of chief mechanical engineer George Jackson Churchward, who was away on holiday at the time – to cut them up. In a stroke, Stanier all but wiped out broad-gauge heritage from the face of the earth.

On his return, Churchward was understandably horrified, and salvaged many of the parts of *North Star*, but could save only the driving wheels from *Lord of the Isles*.

Stanier had no regrets, and repeated his hooligan approach to history when he oversaw the LMS, which in the late 20s had begun to safeguard examples of its most noteworthy classes. Four locomotives, an old Midland Railway 0-6-0, 1856-built No 401, which was withdrawn in 1925 and restored in 1929, Midland 156 class 2-4-0 No 156 (LMS was numbered 1), and Johnson 0-4-4T No 1226, which harked back to 1875, both set aside on withdrawal in 1930, and North London Railway 4-4-0T No 6 were all earmarked for preservation.

However, shortly after he arrived from Swindon, Stanier ordered all four to be scrapped in 1932.

Clearly he was a man who was interested only in the future (and what a shimmering future he brought to his railway) and there were many who shared his contempt for the commonplace and obsolete. Why would, for instance, anyone want to preserve a 1970s fridge or washing machine for posterity, when it would only serve to take up space, and a modern one could probably do the job more efficiently?

Still, this was not excuse for his actions, which must, even by the standards of the day, seem grossly irresponsible. The concept of railway preservation, the

saving of pioneering items for the benefit of future generations, dates back almost to the dawn of the steam railway.

The early Victorians took more care than might at first be supposed to set aside the very earliest locomotives. Isambard Kingdom Brunel's GWR from Paddington to Bristol was still two years in the future when the Canterbury & Whitstable Railway pioneer *Invicta* (the first to work on a public railway south of the Thames) was set aside in 1839, at first kept as a curio in a public park, and now on view in Canterbury Heritage Museum in Stour Street.

Of today's survivors, the next to be retained would be the pioneer from the Stockton & Darlington Railway, *Locomotion No 1*, which was preserved in 1857.

Sadly, Richard Trevithick's 1804 locomotive did not make it. After years of use as a stationary boiler, it ended up among a pile of scrap purchased by the London & North Western Railway. It was put on one side for short time with preservation in mind, until locomotive superintendent, William Webb had a change of heart, and it went to the blast furnace of LNWR's own steelworks.

The GWR was, along with the other major companies of the day, invited in 1925 to take part in celebrations to mark the centenary of the Stockton & Darlington Railway, the world's first public steam-operated line. Suddenly, the directors woke up and realised that they could display no locomotive from their formative years.

The salvaged parts of *North Star* were tracked down and used in the building of a replica at Swindon. It is this locomotive that is today exhibited inside STEAM – Museum of the Great Western Railway at Swindon, although it has never been able to move on its own.

The GWR continued to be unconcerned by any need for preservation, except in the case of No 3440 *City of Truro*, when it was withdrawn in 1931. The locomotive,

Above: The National Railway Museum's replica of Iron Duke. NRM

Opposite: *Fire Fly* runs along a typical stretch of 1850s broad gauge. GWS

Top right: Firefly Trust chairman takes on the role of Isambard Brunel as the new *Fire Fly* is officially launched at Didcot. GWS

Top left: The 21st-century *Fire Fly* in action on its short running line at Didcot Railway Centre. FIREFLY TRUST

Middle right: *Fire Fly* takes on water at Didcot. Its coach is representative of third-class travel in the 1840s. GWS

Middle left: Great Western traction a century apart: the new *Fire Fly* stands at the interchange station in the bay opposite 1930s pioneer diesel-railcar W22. GWS

Bottom right: Cmdr John Mosse about to put the axle into the first *Fire Fly* wheel at Swindon in March 1996. FIREFLY TRUST

Bottom left: Wheelsets for the new *Fire Fly* await fitting at Didcot. FIREFLY TRUST

which the GWR claimed had been the first in the world to top 100mph, is now part of our national collection and under the National Railway Museum returned to the main line in time to celebrate the centenary of that run in 2004.

Despite the considerable celebrations in 1935 marking the GWR's own centenary, the company showed no interest in salvaging any large locomotive relic from the broad-gauge era. South Devon Railway 2-4-0 saddle-tank *Prince*, which had been built in 1871, was among the locomotives converted to standard gauge in 1893 and soldiered on for another six years before its withdrawal in 1899. After that, it was used as a stationary boiler in Swindon Works.

Its rediscovery led to renewed interest in the broad gauge, but nonetheless the GWR saw fit to scrap it.

From late Victorian times, it was clear that the general public had a greater interest in railways than merely travelling on them. The early, crude model trains proved very popular and led to the establishment of manufacturers like Hornby, Marklin and Bassett-Lowke, while miniature, live steam lines at seaside resorts, in parks and pleasure gardens did a roaring trade.

The idea of private individuals taking over a railway to run it independently, or as a place on which heritage traction could be operated (as opposed to being kept in a museum on static display) may have its origins in the abortive attempts to revive the 3ft gauge Southwold Railway in Suffolk after it closed in 1929.

However, the first railway in Britain, and indeed the world, to be revived by volunteers was the 2ft 3in gauge Talyllyn Railway at Tywyn in central Wales, when a Birmingham-based group, led by transport historian Tom Rolt, took restarted public services after it was set to close.

This example was followed in 1954 by volunteer groups who saved the Ffestiniog Railway and Welshpool & Llanfair, and the Bluebell Railway in Sussex followed these narrow-gauge revivals in 1960, closely behind was

the aforementioned Middleton Railway at Leeds – creating Britain's first two standard gauge preserved lines.

The blue touch paper was lit, and we now have more than 100 operational preserved railways in Britain, most offering the chance to travel behind steam, a form of traction finally discarded by British Railways in August 1968. Numerous classic locomotives from the steam age can now be seen again, polished to perfection by the groups who own and run them.

The driving force behind many volunteers is often the desire to recreate scenes from their own 'golden age', when trainspotting was a hugely popular activity among schoolboys of the 50s and 60s, to be found during the long summer holidays at every station and overbridge with their Ian Allan spotters' guides.

As a result, many preserved lines reflect the railways of the post-war period, with others harking back to the Big Four years of 1923-1948 and a select few specialising in the time before them, the pre-Grouping era.

It has been said that if all the preserved railways in the UK were laid end to end, they would stretch from London to Glasgow and beyond. Maybe so, but for so long there was one major quadrant of British railway heritage missing from the preservation portfolio – Brunel broad gauge.

It was in the early 1980s, however, that fresh green broad-gauge shoots began breaking through the soil in the city that Isambard had made his own – Bristol.

Retired Royal Navy Commander John Mosse, was working as consultant architect to British Rail on the restoration of Temple Meads Old Station in 1981, when he came up with the idea of building of a new *Fire Fly*, a replica of the first one, but nonetheless the 63rd member of the ground-breaking class of 2-2-2s.

He soon found that many others shared his enthusiasm, including Leslie Lloyd, then general manager of the Western Region, and his chief mechanical and electrical engineer John Butt.

Above: *Fire Fly* **simmers alongside the Burlescombe station platform at Didcot.**
FIREFLY TRUST

Above Mixed-gauge pointwork on the Didcot broad-gauge demonstration line. ROBIN JONES

They were soon joined by several retired railway engineers including SAS Smith, who as manager of Swindon Works had overseen the construction of Standard 9F No 92220 *Evening Star*, BR's last steam locomotive, in 1960.

The big breakthrough came when Daniel Gooch's original drawings for the Firefly class were found at Paddington.

By 1982 the Firefly Trust was established and fundraising began.

It became clear that much of Gooch's specification would be unacceptable in the safety-conscious modern world, and Gooch's design would need to be modified.

Enforced changes would include the braking, which on the original was not on the engine but on one side of the tender only, and the boiler, which Gooch had designed to be the main longitudinal strength member, while additionally taking all the horizontal drag loads. Nor was there provision for boiler expansion.

The frame was redesigned to act as a support to the boiler rather than the other way round, with boiler expansion being permitted by the introduction of a dummy firebox, which would also take the drag loading. The frame, although considerably stronger than that of Gooch's, would still be true to the appearance of the original.

By 1987, sufficient money had been raised to allow building to start, as a Manpower Services community project, backed by Bristol City Council.

Within a year, the terms of the Manpower Services training schemes were amended and the council decided against further participation.

At the same time, the trust's workshop on the banks of the River Avon was declared unsafe and the occupants were forced to leave. The uncertainty of the future of the project resulted in the loss of a large loan.

Help was at hand in the form of the Great Western Society, a group dedicated to the preservation of everything from the company whose name itself may have been suggested by Isambard. The society offered space in its new locomotive workshop at Didcot Railway Centre, and soon the partly built engine had arrived.

Meanwhile, the National Railway Museum had commissioned a working replica of the first *Iron Duke* in time for the Great Western 150 celebrations in 1985, together with a matching open carriage.

It was built using parts from two standard gauge Austerity 0-6-0 saddle-tanks, a type of basic but powerful locomotive designed for mass production during WWII, and with nearly 100 examples of them in preservation, the potential loss of two was considered to be no detriment to railway heritage.

The new *Iron Duke* was built using modern materials and methods to exactly resemble Gooch's 1847 drawings, complete with exposed wooden lagging (from 1848 onwards, sheet iron was added over the lagging and painted to match the tender).

A short demonstration running line was built at the York museum to allow it to run, and Didcot also built its own broad-gauge track, complete with mixed-gauge section and the transhipment shed from Burlescombe, where in the days of the break of gauge, passengers and goods had to be switched from one train to another.

Retired airline pilot Sam Bee took over as chairman of the Firefly Trust in November 1998, following the untimely death of Cmdr Mosse.

Following the delivery of a new boiler from Israel Newton & Sons of Bradford and successfully steamed, the new *Fire Fly*, built for a cost of around £200,000 over 23 years, not the 13 weeks and £1735 like the original, ran under its own power for the first time at Didcot on 2 March 2005. It was the first new main line steam locomotive to be built in Britain since *Evening Star* 45 years before.

Fire Fly's public debut came at the railway centre on 30 April 2005, launched into traffic by veteran of film, TV and stage, Anton Rogers, to rapturous applause.

The spirit of Brunel and Gooch had returned at last.

Yet will *Fire Fly* ever run anywhere apart from on Didcot's short demonstration line?

Will there ever be a fully fledged broad-gauge railway in the preservation world?

Previous suggestions to add a broad gauge running rail to today's South Devon Railway between Buckfastleigh and Totnes, a line originally built to 7ft 0¼in gauge, and on the Cholsey & Wallingford Railway near Didcot, came to nothing.

However, as the phenomenal interest shown in the 2006 celebrations to mark the bicentenary of Isambard's birth have shown, there is ever-increasing admiration on a global scale for his many unique works and achievements. Rather than be 'just another preserved steam line' a Brunel broad-gauge railway would allow a fuller glimpse into that fantastic age of change, and could become a major crowd puller or the basis for a Victorian theme park.

To bring such a scheme to reality, however, it would take lorryloads of cash, and an entrepreneur who is broad minded in more ways than one. Much like Isambard Kingdom Brunel.

Bringing Brunel back down to size

MODELLING THE BROAD GAUGE

Above: Modeller Paul Marchese's superb 7mm scale layout of Edgware Road, shows just what can be achieved. It depicts the meeting between the GWR and Metropolitan Railway and features GWR broad-gauge 2-4-0T *Locust*, Metropolitan standard gauge 4-4-0T *Hercules*, and an unfinished carriage posed using a false back scene, which was a real photograph of Edgware Road before completion of the line.

One of the most popular hobbies over the past century has been railway modelling, and it continues to grow apace, with hundreds of splendid models available off-the-shelf, from market-leading manufacturers such as Hornby, Bachmann and Dapol.

However, the development of model railways from crude wind-up toys to beautifully detailed scale models is a 20th-century phenomenon, whereas broad gauge was born and killed off in the 19th.

Unlike standard-gauge types, no ready-to-run models are available at your local store. Therefore, if you would like a Brunel broad-gauge layout of your own for your bedroom, attic or garage, you must build it all yourself – from scratch.

Don't despair; for there are experts on hand, not only to help you with practical advice, but also to supply you with a range of wonderfully crafted model kits.

The Broad Gauge Society was formed in 1980 by modellers with an interest in the Brunel system. Its aims are to provide practical and detailed information about modelling 7ft 0¼in gauge and establish essential supplies to kit builders.

A twice-yearly magazine, *The Broadsheet*, disseminates essential information to modellers and historians alike, with data sheets covering almost every example of rolling stock that ran on Brunel's system.

The society has produced ranges of etched brass and white metal kits, in both 4mm and 7mm to 1ft scales - including the essential bridge rail in both scales, and many of them can be built by an enthusiastic, seasoned modeller with a medium skill level.

An annual field trip to an area of broad gauge interest is held by the society, with a view to rediscovering artefacts from this great, often forgotten era of our railway heritage. Members are often amazed by how much still survives.

Of course, the biggest drawback to building any model railway layout is space, and this accounts for the popularity of the 2mm to the foot, or N gauge, over the past 30 years.

If you want to build a Brunel layout in 4mm scale (O gauge), you need track with rails 28mm wide – almost as big as O gauge (7mm) that has 32mm track.

If you opt for O scale, you need track with railways 50mm apart. But where do those graceful, wide curves go, and who has the space available?

Nonetheless, a surprising number of modellers do try their hand at broad gauge, often with hugely satisfying results. Occasionally, their layouts can be seen at model exhibitions.

The society's locomotive, carriage and wagon kits largely cover the later broad-gauge period, post-1860, but if do you want to go back to the earlier decades, you will have to go back to the time-honoured modelling basics, and scratch build, using plastic, card and balsa wood, although the society can still help you in a big way, by supplying wheels, axle boxes, buffers and other castings.

Several makers of parts for OO and O gauge kit builders now also supply some components for post-1860, broad-gauge models.

The big advantage with this later period of the Brunel system is that as the cut-off date of 1892 for the 7ft 0¼in gauge approached, Swindon Works turned out more locomotive carriage and wagon designs and components, which could be converted to narrow gauge when necessary.

Some of these coaches took only half an hour to convert to 4ft 8½in gauge and ran on the GWR for many years afterwards.

Therefore, the door is wide open for the modeller to 'back convert' proprietary standard-gauge kits, from specialist makers to represent broad gauge in an authentic manner. Again, the society supplies suitable 'wide ends' for such tabletop, modern-day coach conversions.

Modelling the later period of broad gauge is helped greatly by the huge amount of quality photographs that were taken on glass plates, recording very fine detail. By contrast, many of the sketches of the Brunel system in its infancy may have great artistic merit but in terms of

scale and technical usefulness, are non-starters.

Track building, however, presents the biggest problem – and with broad gauge, you will have to build it yourself – it is the exact opposite of opening that OO gauge Christmas present and having it running around the lounge within minutes.

If you have the skill, you could even try mixed gauge, which opens up a wealth of possibilities.

Models can never be a substitute for the prototype in preservation, but as virtually everything was lost after 1892 in terms of track, engines and rolling stock, it is the best we can do. As you can see from the magnificent recreations on these pages, building your own Brunel system can be hugely rewarding.

The Broad Gauge Society, which provided the photographs on these pages, can be contacted via membership secretary, Hugh Smith, 31b, Carnarvon Road, Stratford, London, E15 4JW, email: hugh.slimgit@talk21.com

It can provide details of other specialist manufacturers of broad-gauge products and components. Its website is www.broadgauge.org.uk

Above: An Armstrong convertible 0-6-0 tender engine, built by Alan Garner from a Scorpio Models kit.

Below: Broad-gauge aficionado Brian Arman built this superb model of *Plato* from the society's kit for a Banking Class 0-6-0ST of 1852/4.

Top: The West Country fish trade became important towards the end of the broad-gauge era and seven of these impressive bogie fish trucks were built in 1889 to cater for the expanding traffic. The unusual design showcases the major differences between standard gauge and the Brunel broad gauge, which was in a way, a different form of transport all of its own. This model is built from a Broad Gauge Society kit.

Above right: A low-level shot of the Edgware Road layout.

Right: The bonnet-ended tilt wagons were a distinctive part of the Brunel broad-gauge scene from the earliest days and many lasted until the end in 1892. Society member Alan Garner built this model of an iron-tilt wagon from a Victorian Models kit.

Bottom right: Broad Gauge Society member Nick Saltzman models Brunel's broad gauge in 3mm scale, made popular by Tri-ang TT (tabletop) gauge in the 1950s. This unpainted model of a Bristol & Exeter Railway 4-2-4WT was built from scratch and is seen running on his exhibition layout, Bagborough West.

A year
of inspiration

Pick of the main events celebrating the bicentenary of the birth of Isambard Kingdom Brunel in 2006.
For more details, also see the Brunel 200 website www.brunel200.com

APRIL

Until autumn	Brunel and the *Great Eastern* – Wonder of the World	Exhibition about Brunel's *Great Eastern*, which laid the first successful Atlantic telegraph cable – under the guidance of his former locomotive superintendent Daniel Gooch – with models and fittings from the ship. Porthcurno Telegraph Museum, Eastern House, Porthcurno, Cornwall, TR19 6JX. Tel: 01736 810966. Web: www.porthcurno.org.uk
1-31 October	Nine Lives of IK Brunel and professional life.	Major exhibition at the *SS Great Britain* in Bristol's Floating Harbour exploring Brunel's private Exhibits include the National Railway Museum's replica GWR broad gauge *Iron Duke* from York. An actor in costume meets visitors to the Brunel 200 exhibition and the *SS Great Britain* on 8, 9, 14, 15 and 29 April. Tel: 0117 926 0680 Web: www.ssgreatbritain.org
1-30	Deserving of Wonder – the Triumphs of Brunel	Exhibition at Bristol Central Library of photographs by David White of Brunel's greatest engineering triumphs, taken with the same 19th century camera and lens combination as Robert Howlett used for the classic shot of Brunel as seen in our Great Eastern section.
2-29	Bridge exhibition	Inspired by Brunel, a collaborative exhibition between Bristol School of Art, Media and Design and Bristol's design agencies, looking at the creative talent within the city today. Royal West of England Academy, Queen's Road, Clifton, Bristol BS8 1PX. Tel. 0117 9735129 Web: www.rwa.org.uk
4-27	Hats Off to Brunel exhibition	Bristol's suburbs of Hotwells and Cliftonwood mark Brunel 200 with a multi-media exhibition of work produced by local artists around a Brunel theme at Bristol's CREATE Centre, located in one of the three large redbrick tobacco warehouses in Cumberland Basin. Web: www.visitbristol.co.uk/site/things_to_do/a-z/c/p_24741
7	Institute of Civil Engineers Southern's Brunel	Unveiling of monument to Brunel by the Lord Mayor of Portsmouth at 11.30am followed by lecture, Brunel, His Achievements and His Legacy at Portsmouth University.
8	Clifton Suspension Bridge lighting launch	New lights illuminating the bridge switched on, a celebratory firework display; excerpts from a community play, Bristol Choral Society and a recitation of Ralph Hoyte's epic Brunel poem.
8	Brunel Anniversary Ltd Portsmouth event	GWR express passenger locomotive No 6024 *King Edward I* hauls a special train from Bristol Temple Meads to Shrewsbury. Contact Kingfisher Railtours on 0870 747 2983.
8-9	Brunel's birthday and major exhibitions at STEAM	STEAM – Museum of the Great Western Railway at Swindon – special family weekend of celebrations including a steam fairground. Also, launch of Brunel and the Battle of the Gauges an exhibition running until 30 September, with reconstruction of Brunel's 18 Duke Street office. STEAM, Kemble Drive, Swindon, Wiltshire SN2 2TA Tel: 01796 466646. Web: www.steam-museum.org.uk
8-9	Birthday weekend celebrations, Bristol	Activities include arts projects, steam train and steam boat tours. Tel: 01454 888686
8-9	British Empire and Commonwealth Museum	Brunel's original Temple Meads station reopens to the public for the first time since its recent restoration. A guide tour highlights the massive passenger shed, cavernous underground vaults and the mock-Gothic grandeur of the GWR boardroom. Tours will then take place on two Sundays of each month until October, pre-booking essential. Also, from early April to late summer, the museum will mount displays about the GWR and Temple Meads, with guided walks and ferryboat rides between and around the Brunel sites, and events including family fun days, talks, 'engineering challenges', performances and workshops. Tel: 0117 925 4980.
9	Brunel Anniversary Ltd	GWR No 6024 *King Edward I* hauls a special train from Bristol Temple Meads to Hereford.
9	Powderham Castle Brunel birthday celebrations	Brunel negotiated for his South Devon Railway to run through the grounds of this castle on the A379 south of Exeter, which has its own miniature railway and will be offering rides as well as

Above: Built in the 1850s, Brunel Manor in the Watcombe area of Torquay was to have been the retirement home of Isambard Kingdom Brunel. Although he died in 1859 and never had the chance to live in it, the house and gardens with their magnificent sea views retain some of his original design. In 1962, Brunel Manor was bought by the Woodlands House of Prayer Trust. To coincide with the birthday celebrations, the manor is opening the gardens on selected occasions in 2006, and is holding other Brunel-inspired events including painting breaks. Tel: 01803 329333. Web: www.brunelmanor.com
SOVEREIGN

		guided tours during a day-long celebration of his life and works. Tel: 01626 890243
9	Brunel's broad gauge birthday steaming Brunel 200 tours	Special gala day at Didcot Railway Centre with the award-winning replica GWR *Fire Fly* locomotive and its coach steaming on broad gauge demonstration track. Note: *Fire Fly* will steam on selected dates throughout 2006 – contact the Great Western Society for more details. Tel: 01235 817200. Web: www.didcotrailwaycentre.org.uk
9-2 July	Brunel in Bath	Exhibition and events programme outlining the story of the GWR and its impact on Bath. Holburne Museum, Great Pulteney Street, Bath BA2 4DB. Tel: 01225 466669.
9	Brunel's Birthday at Thames Tunnel	The Brunel Engine House, Rotherhithe. Tel: 020 7231 3840 for details of this and other special events throughout the year, including tunnel tours.
9	Brunel Remembered	Outdoor re-enactment at 2pm, covering selected periods from Brunel's life, with Royal Albert Bridge in background. Ashtorre Rock Centre, Waterside, Saltash. Tel: 01752 844255.
9	Brunel exhibition and birthday tea at Brunel Manor	The retirement home of IK Brunel he never saw finished. Free public opening of the gardens until 14 April. Brunel Manor, Teignmouth Road, Torquay TQ1 4SF. Tel: 01803 329333 Web: www.brunelmanor.com
9-29 September	Brunel model railway exhibition	Pendon Museum, Long Wittenham, Abingdon, Oxfordshire, OX14 4QD. Tel: 01865 407365. Broad gauge guest layouts on 10-11 June.
9	Lighting of Western Arches,	Chippenham. Tel: 01249 706333.
9-30 September	Brunel at Brixham	Exhibition at Brixham Museum of Brunel's part in the development of the South Devon port.
10 (opens)	Brunel, Brotherhood and the Railway	Exhibition about local contractor Rowland Brotherhood's partnership with Brunel and their affect on Chippenham. Chippenham Museum and Heritage Centre, 10 Market Place, Chippenham, SN15 3HF. Tel: 01249 705020.
12	Brunel and the GWR	A showing of the TV South West archive film. Ashtorre Rock community centre, Waterside, Saltash. Tel: 01752 844255.
13	Show of Strength's An Audience with Sarah Guppy	Sarah Guppy (1770-1852), a Bristol-based designer, was an innovator ahead of her time. She patented a method for making safe piling for bridges in 1811, seven years before Telford's Menai Bridge, and when Brunel was aged five. Other patents were for a tea and coffee urn (1812), an exercise bed (1831) and a method for caulking ships (1844). Although older than Brunel, she died just seven years before him and worked until at least 1844, when she was 74. In this lecture/theatre performance, 'Guppy' talks about her life and work, including her significant links with Brunel, illustrated with her designs, recreated in 3D by students working from her original patents and drawings.City of Bristol College. Tel: 0117 312 5000.
15-18 June	Brunel and the Art of Invention	A major exhibition of nationally important artworks at Bristol's City Museum and Art Gallery highlighting the creative links between art, science and industry. Artworks on loan will include William Powell Frith's magnificent large-scale canvas *The Railway Station* showing travellers embarking on the Great Western Railway from Paddington. Bristol's City Museum & Art Gallery, Queen's Road, Bristol, BS8 1RL. Tel: 0117 922. 3571
20- 21	Modern Voyages: Sea Travel since Brunel	Academic conference on sea travel since Brunel, at SS *Great Britain*. University of Bristol Department of History of Art, 43 Woodland Road Bristol BS8 1UU. Tel: 0117 331 1197.
20–22	Castles in the Air	From his parent's romantic meeting in the shadow of the guillotine, to his untimely demise, Castles in the Air, a major musical and theatrical event at Bristol Industrial Museum's L shed on the Floating Harbour, retells the story of Isambard's life. Tel: 0117 925 1470.
26	Brunel in postcards	Presentation of antiquarian postcards of Brunel structures. Ashtorre Rock community centre, Waterside, Saltash. Tel: 01752 844255.
30	Swindon Railway Village guided walks	English Heritage series of guided tours of Swindon Railway Village, also being staged on 28 May, 25 June, 30 July, 27 August, 24 September. Tel: 01793 414797.

MAY

May	Atmospheric watercolours	The newly reopened Newton Abbot Town & GWR Museum at 2a St Pauls Road will display the original William Dawson watercolours of Brunel's atmospheric railway depicting the line from Exeter to Totnes, on loan from the Institution of Civil Engineers. Tel: 01626 201121.
1	Brunel returns to Dawlish	'IK Brunel' arrives at Dawlish station, to take part in a procession from the seafront to the museum for the new Dawlish and Brunel exhibition – in Barton Terrace – which runs until 30 September. Tel: 01626 888557
4	Brunel Celebration and Underground Geology of London	The Brunel Anniversary Symposium – the Engineering Geology of London Tunnels. Proposed field trip to the Brunel Engine House at Rotherhithe and the Thames Tunnel. Run by Natural History Museum. Tel: 0207 942 5000.
11	Recreation of the Royal Dinner of 1843	Academic event at British Empire & Commonwealth Museum. Government chief scientific officer Lord Sainsbury will give an address on the future of engineering. Tel: 0117 925 4980.
13-14	Atmospheric Brunel festival, Forde House, Newton Abbot	Exhibition of Brunel and GWR artefacts in the home of Teignbridge District Council, including a section of atmospheric pipe, plus a Brunel community play run by Wren Music of Okehampton. Demonstrations of the working atmospheric railway from Barometer World – as seen in our Atmospheric Caper section – and vacuum guns and hemispheres. Tel: 01626 201121.
15-15 July	Brunel art exhibition at Falmouth	Major exhibition about Brunel's achievements in Cornwall, including rare Cornish prints, photographs, archives and paintings, at Falmouth Art Gallery. Tel: 01326 313863.
29	Steam back to Box	The village of Box at the western end of Brunel's tunnel celebrates his bicentenary with the return of steam in the form of Severn Valley Railway-based GWR prairie tank No 4566 for static display in the village as the centrepiece of festivities.

JUNE

10-30 September	Brunel exhibition at Torquay Museum	Exhibition at the Babbacombe Road museum highlighting the growth of the seaside resort following the building of Brunel's broad gauge line. Tel: 01803 293975.
24-2 July	Brunel festivities in Portsmouth	Activities in Brunel's birthplace include talks by Adam Hart Davies, performance of a play by Timothy West and music from Evelyn Glennie. Tel: 023 9268 1390.
24-3 July	Brunel on stamps	A display of IK Brunel as portrayed on stamps, at Powderham Castle near Exeter. Tel: 01626 890243.
26-28	Brunel University International Conference: Advances in Bridge Engineering	School of Engineering and Design, Brunel University, Uxbridge, Middlesex UB8 3PH. Tel: 01895 266962.

JULY

1-7	Trains, Planes and Automobiles	Film event at the Science Museum, Wroughton, Wiltshire, celebrating 200 years of technological innovation in Swindon. Tel: 01793 846200.
5	Bicentenary special	Institute of Civil Engineers and Newcomen Society private steam-hauled main line train from Paddington to Bristol for the Brunel Bicentenary Conference behind GWR express passenger locomotive No 6024 *King Edward I*.
6-7	Brunel bicentenary conference	Academic event at the British Commonwealth & Empire Museum. Speakers include Sir Neil Cossons, chairman of English Heritage and John Armitt, chief executive of Network Rail. Contact: ICE Conferences. Tel: 0207 665 2313.
7-16	Brunel Festival in Swindon	Huge community-based event, featuring: 7-8: Building Bridges – Swindon talent showcasing performances at the Wyvern Theatre; 11-14: lunchtime performances under the canopies on the Parade in the town centre; 15: Brunel carnival parade day of street theatre, comedy and music; 16: Crossing the Great Divide (in Faringdon Park and the Railway Village) – performances and children's activities; 16: Festival Finale in Faringdon Park. Tel: 01793 530328. Web: www.swindonbrunel200.co.uk
18	Smeaton Lecture	Historian Steven Brindle talks about Brunel, ICE, London. Tel: 0207 222 7722.
19	*SS Great Britain* anniversary	Celebrations around Bristol's Floating Harbour marking the anniversary of launch of *SS Great Britain*.
7– 4 September	The Railway Comes to Town	Exhibition telling the story of the transformation of Swindon from a sleepy village to a dynamic industrial town.
Late July	**Bristol Harbour Festival with Brunel-themed events.**	

AUGUST

5	Brunel at Paignton	'Brunel' to appear on Paignton Green during Paignton Regatta, courtesy of Torquay Museum.
15	Brunel at Paignton	'Brunel' actor travelling on Paignton & Dartmouth Steam Railway, which was built as a broad gauge line and surveyed by him.

SEPTEMBER

7-8	BA Festival of Science	ICE East of England event in Norwich. Programme includes a debate at Norwich City Football Club: 'This house believes that there has never since been a civil engineer of the stature of Brunel', chaired by Gordon Masterton. Gala dinner to follow. Tel: 020 7222 7722.
16-17	Swindon Railway Festival	The annual event at Swindon's STEAM Museum pays tribute to the great engineer who shaped the town's future. Web: www.steam-museum.org.uk
16-17	Swindon & Cricklade Railway steam weekend	Brunel 200 gala event at Swindon's own preserved railway, at Blundson station. Tel: 01793 771615.
16-17	Brunel: The Little Man in the Tall Hat	The Janice Thompson Performance Trust premieres newly commissioned youth opera. More than 100 young people set off on the annual 'Swindon Trip'. On their journey they bring to life the story and achievements of Brunel and celebrate the rich history of Swindon's singing and music making, which started in its Railway Village and continues to flourish in the town. St Mark's church, Railway Village, Swindon. Tel: 01793 530328. Web: www.swindonbrunel200.co.uk
22-24	Brunel quilts	Exhibition by Weston Quilters, a display of specially made quilts providing individual interpretations of the life and work of Isambard Kingdom Brunel. Winter Gardens in Weston-Super-Mare. Tel: 01934 417117.
September	Illumination of Brunel's Royal Albert Bridge, Saltash (date to be confirmed). Tel: 01752 304849.	

This is by no means a complete listing of all events, with many more being held on a local basis. For further details contact Tourist Information Offices at Bristol, tel: 0117 926 0767, Bath, tel: 01225 477101 or Swindon, tel: 01793 530328.